The Little Book

of

Buddhist Meditation

Establishing a daily meditation practice

by Eric K. Van Horn

CreateSpace Independent Publishing Platform

ISBN-13: 978-1523938865

ISBN-10: 1523938862

First Edition 2016 (1)

Revised 2017 (2)

Dedicated to the monks and nuns

Of the monastic Saṇgha

Who have so selflessly preserved

And practiced the Buddha’s teachings

For the last 2500 years.

"'The safe and good path to be traveled joyfully' is a term for the Noble Eight Book Path."

The Little Books on Buddhism series:

Book 1: *The Little Book of Buddhist Meditation: Establishing a daily meditation practice*

Book 2: *The Little Book on Buddhist Virtue: The Buddha's teachings on happiness through skillful conduct*

Book 3: *The Little Book of the Life of the Buddha*

Book 4: *The Little Book of Buddhist Wisdom: The Buddha's teachings on the Four Noble Truths, the three marks of existence, causality, and karma*

Book 5: *The Little Book of Buddhist Mindfulness & Concentration*

Book 6: *The Little Book of Buddhist Daily Living: The Discipline for Lay People*

Book 7: *The Little Book of Buddhist Rebirth*

Book 8: *The Little Book of Buddhist Awakening: The Buddha's instructions on attaining enlightenment*

Also by this author:

The Travel Guide to the Buddha's Path

Table of Contents

Preface

Train in acts of merit
that yield the foremost profit of
bliss –
develop generosity,
a life in tune,
a mind of good will.
Developing these
three things
that bring about bliss,
the wise reappear
in a world of bliss
unalloyed.
- [Iti 1.22]

When I wrote my first book on Buddhist practice, *The Travel Guide to the Buddha's Path,* it was with the intention of tracing the entire arc of the Buddha's training from the first time that you sit down in meditation until you attain the first level of awakening, which is called "stream-entry." I believe that it accomplished that task. However, being that the Buddha's teachings are quite extensive and that they cover a lot of ground, many people found that volume a little overwhelming.

In response to that criticism, I am using that book as a basis for a series of smaller volumes, ones that will tackle one subject at a time. In that way the Buddhist path is broken down into smaller, more palatable chunks. It also serves the purpose of permitting people who may be strong in one area but weak in another to concentrate on topics that are appropriate for them. And finally, it enables each volume to be taught as a course in that one subject.

So this is the first volume in the *Little Books on Buddhism Series*. It will eventually cover all of the ground in *The Travel Guide to the Buddha's Path,* as noted, in smaller pieces, and it is also organized somewhat differently. In some cases these smaller volumes will also expand on what is in *The Travel Guide*.

This volume is for the beginning meditator. However, because meditation is taught in so many different ways, it may serve the experienced meditator as well. I have seen many people who practiced diligently for many years, and who never really seemed to make much progress. Meditation is a skill. It is like learning a craft. The Buddha himself often used crafts in his similes about meditation.

I am often surprised – and dismayed – at how many sincere, experienced meditators seem to meditate because it is something they feel they have to do, rather than something they want to do. Meditation should be enjoyable. It will, of course, not always be that way, but on the whole the practice of meditation should help you establish a sense of well-being, confidence, serenity, and peace of mind.

Yes, at times it will be work. Ṭhānissaro Bhikkhu, the abbot of Metta Forest Monastery in Valley Center, California, compares it to playing basketball. There is effort, of course, but you should be enjoying it. Otherwise there is no point. If you learn to love meditation, then you will do it because you want to do it and because you like to do it. And on those days where it is a struggle, you can chalk it up to a difficult day, but there is always the next sitting.

Some years ago I did a solo retreat at the Embracing Simplicity Hermitage in Asheville, North Carolina. At the end of the week I was talking to the resident monk there, Bhikkhu Pannadipa, and I told him that it occurred to me during the week that I could not always be sure when I was "making progress." Everyone enjoys those calm, serene periods of meditation. But it is quite possible that those are just rest times for the mind, and the real work happens during the difficult sittings.

The Buddha's message is timeless. The human mind has not changed in the 2400 years that have passed since his death. The people who show up in the Buddhist literature are all too familiar. The struggles of the people are just as familiar. And the Buddha's understanding of the transcendent nature of reality has not changed, either. There have been many attempts to shoehorn the Buddha's teachings into a narrow, Western, cultural context. But not only is that unnecessary, it corrupts his beautiful understanding of the path to greater happiness and final liberation. This Little Book is a gateway to what I hope will be a long and fruitful journey along that path for you.

Eric Van Horn
Rio Rancho, New Mexico
6-Feb-2016
nobleeightfoldblog.com

Preface to the Revised Edition

I have been working my way through all of the books that I have written, reviewing what I wrote, double checking everything with what the Buddha taught, making minor stylistic changes to make everything uniform, and making occasional content changes to reflect a slightly better understanding or to express things in a way that I hope will be clearer. And as I have been doing this, I ran across a passage that quite struck me. The following rendering is from the "Sampasādanīya Sutta: Serene Faith" [DN 28].

The situation is a conversation between the Buddha and one of his chief disciples, Sāriputta. It begins with Sāriputta making this declaration:

"It is clear to me, Lord, that there never has been, never will be and is not now another ascetic or brahmin who is better or more enlightened than the Lord."

Sāriputta was trying to pay the Buddha a compliment. Somewhat surprisingly, the Buddha challenged Sāriputta, and he did it quite aggressively. He asked Sāriputta rather pointedly, "How do you know? How can you make such an assertion?"

"You have spoken boldly with a bull's voice, Sāriputta, you have roared the lion's roar of certainty. How is this? Have all the arahant Buddhas of the past appeared to you, and were the minds of all those Lords open to you, so as to say: 'These Lords were of such virtue, such was their teaching, such their wisdom, such their way, such their liberation?'"

"No, Lord."

"And have you perceived all the arahant Buddhas who will appear in the future?"

"No, Lord."

"Well then, Sāriputta, you know me as the arahant Buddha, and do you know: 'The Lord is of such virtue, such his teaching, such his wisdom, such his way, such his liberation?'"

"No, Lord."

"So, Sāriputta, you do not have knowledge of the minds of the Buddhas of the past, the future or the present. Then, Sāriputta, have you not spoken boldly with a bull's voice and roared the lion's roar of certainty with your declaration?"

I mean, wow. Sāriputta was an arahant. He had attained a full awakening. The Buddha named him as one of his two chief disciples. In the sutta "Foremost," the Buddha declared, "Bhikkhus, the foremost of my bhikkhu disciples with great wisdom is Sāriputta" [AN 1.189]. This seems like pretty harsh treatment for someone who was trying to say something nice.

But Sāriputta was unfazed. Given that he was an arahant, this is not surprising. He gave this poetic, extraordinary reply:

"Lord, the minds of the arahant Buddhas of the past, future and present are not open to me. But I know the drift of the Dhamma. Lord, it is as if there were a royal frontier city, with mighty bastions and a mighty encircling wall in which was a single gate, at which was a gatekeeper, wise, skilled and clever, who kept out strangers and let in those he knew. And he, constantly patrolling and following along a path, might not see the joins and clefts in the bastion, even such as a cat might creep through. But whatever larger creatures entered or left the city, must all go through this very gate. And it seems to me, Lord, that the drift of the Dhamma is the same. All those arahant Buddhas of the past attained to supreme enlightenment by abandoning the five hindrances, defilements of mind which weaken understanding, having firmly established the four foundations of mindfulness in their minds, and realized the seven factors of enlightenment as they really are. All the arahant Buddhas of the future will do likewise, and you, Lord, who are now the arahant, fully-enlightened Buddha, have done the same."

There are so many lovely phrases here. He began by saying that he knew "the drift of the Dhamma." "Drift" indicates "flow." He knew how and where the Dhamma flows. He understood its properties and characteristics. He knew where it came from and where it goes.

And then he said that understanding the flow of the Dhamma, he knew that anyone who becomes a Buddha, must become a Buddha by using the same path. His comparison was to a fortress with only one entrance. He knew that anyone who came into the fortress must come that way.

I am pointing out this passage, because as you either know now or may discover, when I write about the Dharma, it is rooted in the

Buddha's original teachings. And that is not because of some ideological approach or scholastic approach or rigid orthodoxy. The Buddha himself would not have a very high opinion of that.

It is because through many years of study and practice, I have come to have a deep faith and trust in what he taught. As the scholars like to say, the Pāli Canon is "coherent and cogent." It is compelling in its breadth and depth. But it is not just the words, it is when they are put into practice that such powerful and sometimes astonishing results can happen. And the more you read, and the more you understand, and the more you practice, the deeper your understanding grows. And the more that happens, the more you appreciate the priceless gift that is the Buddha's teachings.

But what this passage in particular says to me is that to gain entry to the fortress, to attain awakening and to be free from stress and suffering, there is only one way to get there, and that is the Dhamma and Discipline that the Buddha taught. Accept no substitutes.

To be sure, the Buddha never told anyone that they had to do anything. But what he did say was that if you want a certain result, this is how to get it. The Mettā Sutta [AN 11.15] famously begins:

> *This is what should be done*
> *By one who is skilled in goodness*
> *And who knows the path of peace.*

I heard a story about a retreat on the Mettā Sutta where they spent the whole morning hung up on the word "should" in this passage. Now, the Buddha didn't say "you have to do this." But what he said is that this is what you should do *if* you want to be "skilled in goodness and know the path of peace."

If you want to run a marathon, you can't sit around and watch TV all day. And the Buddha didn't say that if you do sit around and watch TV all day that you are a bad person, or you will go to hell, or anything like that. He was simply saying that if you want to run a marathon, there are some things you have to do. And in this case, if you want to be happier and more skillful and eventually to become free from stress and suffering, here is what you should do.

But it is also implied in this simile to be wary of con artists and revisionists, of snake oil salesmen (and presumably women as well) who are selling you a cheap facsimile. Sadly there are many of them in the Buddhist world today. If you follow any of them too closely, you are never going to get into the fortress. There is only one way in. You may wander quite happily in the forest for a while, but inevitably some gazelle will have you for lunch. Something will go wrong in your life or in your practice, and it will all fall apart. Or you will realize that you have been going to retreats and spending time and effort and money for years, and you really have not gotten anywhere at all.

The good news is that with diligence and sincerity, the instructions are all there. OK, so it's a big instruction guide. That just means that you won't run out of things to do. There is always more to learn. You won't get bored. And the really, really good news is that there is a way in. The Buddha has gotten in, he knows how to get there, and he left us a map of how to do it for ourselves.

Eric Van Horn
Rio Rancho, New Mexico
17-Jun-2017

Terminology and Conventions

Because the Buddhist Canon that I use is in the Pāli language, I usually use Pāli terms. However, some Sanskrit Buddhist terms have become common in the English language, and it seems rather affected not to use them. The two most obvious examples are the words "nirvāṇa," which is "nibbāna" in Pāli, and "Dharma," which is "Dhamma" in Pāli. For the most part I use the commonly known terms. But if it seems awkward to have the Pāli terms in quotes or in certain words (like "Dhammacakkappavattana") and use the Sanskrit terms in the main text, I use the Pāli words.

I try to avoid technical terms in the beginning of the guide until you can get used to them. However, if there are terms with which you are unfamiliar, they should be in the glossary in Appendix A.

As per APA style guidelines, book names are italicized (i.e., *Foundations of Buddhism*) and magazine articles and Internet resources are capitalized and quoted (i.e., "The Benefits of Walking Meditation").

Internet Conventions

There are many references to resources that are on the Internet. This is always a problem because hyperlinks are notoriously unreliable. Thus, I have adopted a convention of putting Internet search keywords in the text. For example, a reference to Thich Nhat Hanh's gāthās ("poems") is "thich nhat hanh gathas here and now." If you do an Internet search with your browser, the first item in the search results should be the appropriate resource.

The other case is when an article is sighted. It will look like this:

- [Sayadaw U Silananda, "The Benefits of Walking Meditation"]

Searching on the author's name and the article name should get you to the article. Some names and words use diacritical marks, and you may have to remove them to find the correct resource. For example, for the name "Ṭhānissaro" use the non-diacritical form "Thanissaro."

Abbreviations for Pāli Text References

AN: *Aṅguttara Nikāya, The Numerical Discourses of the Buddha*

Bv: *Buddhavaṃsa, Chronicle of Buddhas*

BvA: *Buddhavaṃsatthakathā,* commentary to the *Buddhavaṃsa*

Cv: *Cullavagga,* the *"smaller book,"* the second volume in the *Khandhaka,* which is the second book of the monastic code (the *Vinaya*)

Dhp: *Dhammapada, The Path of Dhamma,* a collection of 423 verses

DhpA: *Dhammapada-aṭṭhakathā,* commentary to the *Dhammapada*

DN: *Digha Nikāya, The Long Discourses of the Buddha*

Iti: *Itivuttaka, This Was Said* (by the Buddha), Sayings of the Buddha

Ja: *Jātaka Tales,* previous life stories of the Buddha

JaA: *Jātaka-aṭṭhakathā,* commentary on the *Jātaka Tales*

Khp: *Khuddakapāṭha, Short Passages*

MA: *Majjhima Nikāya Aṭṭhakathā,* commentary on *The Middle Length Discourses of the Buddha* (by Buddhaghosa)

MN: *Majjhima Nikāya, The Middle Length Discourses of the Buddha*

Mv: *Mahāvagga,* the first volume in the *Khandhaka,* which is the second book of the monastic code (the *Vinaya*)

Pm: *Pātimokkha, The Code of Monastic Discipline,* the first book of the monastic code (the *Vinaya*)

SN: *Saṃyutta Nikāya, The Connected Discourses of the Buddha*

S Nip: *Sutta Nipāta, The Sutta Collection,* literally, "suttas falling down," a sutta collection in the *Khuddaka Nikāya* consisting mostly of verse

Sv: *Sutta-vibhaṅga: Classification of the Suttas,* the "origin stories" for the Pātimokkha rules

Thag: *Theragāthā*: *Verses of the Elder Monks*

ThagA: *Theragāthā-aṭṭhakathā*: commentary to the *Theragāthā*

Thig: *Therīgāthā*: *Verses of the Elder Nuns*

ThigA: *Therīgāthā-aṭṭhakathā*: commentary to the *Therīgāthā*

Ud: *Udana, Exclamations,* the third book of the *Khuddaka Nikāya*

Vin: *Vinaya Pitaka, Basket of Discipline,* the monastic rules for monks and nuns.

Introduction

"And what is the noble search? Here someone being himself subject to birth, having understood the danger in what is subject to birth, seeks the unborn supreme security from bondage, Nibbāna; being himself subject to aging, having understood the danger in what is subject to aging, he seeks the unaging supreme security from bondage, Nibbāna; being himself subject to sickness, having understood the danger in what is subject to sickness, he seeks the unailing supreme security from bondage, Nibbāna; being himself subject to death, having understood the danger in what is subject to death, he seeks the deathless supreme security from bondage, Nibbāna; being himself subject to sorrow, having understood the danger in what is subject to sorrow, he seeks the sorrowless supreme security from bondage, Nibbāna; being himself subject to defilement, having understood the danger in what is subject to defilement, he seeks the undefiled supreme security from bondage, Nibbāna. This is the noble search."
- [MN 26.12]

This is the first in a series of lessons that will teach you how to meditate. This type of meditation is based on the Buddha's original teachings. The Buddha himself either gave these instructions, or they are in the spirit of what he taught. (I will try and point out which ones are which as we proceed.) The source for what the Buddha taught is the Pāli Canon. Pāli is a language of ancient India. The Pāli Canon is at present the best and most complete source we have for the Buddha's original teachings.

You do not have to be a Buddhist to benefit from the Buddha's teachings. Many of his teachings are non-sectarian and can be of benefit to anyone. So if you find some aspect of the Buddha's teaching to be a problem, you can put it aside for now. The best thing that you can do with a teaching that you find difficult to accept or do not understand is to file it away for future reference.

The Buddha taught a path that is called "sīla-samādhi-pañña." "Sīla" is the Pāli word for morality, virtue, or right conduct. "Samādhi" is the Pāli word for concentration or mental absorption. And "pañña" is the Pāli word for wisdom, or discernment.

Normally, the first teaching in Buddhism is sīla. However, I think that in the West there are some problems with teaching morality first, so I will begin with the practice of samādhi. The purpose of samādhi is to establish a sense of well-being. It is your home base. You go there whenever you are struggling. In its purest form the Buddha called this the "pleasure born of seclusion." Once we have discussed how to establish well-being, we will discuss the Buddha's teachings on virtue.

The Purpose of Buddhist Meditation

The Buddha famously said, "...both formerly and now what I teach is suffering and the cessation of suffering" [MN 22.38, SN 22.86]. This is very useful to remember. Sometimes it seems that one part of the path is in conflict with another part of the path. In these cases, remember that the basic premise of what the Buddha taught is to end suffering.

One of the beauties of the Buddha's path is that it is not an all or nothing proposition. You do not have to wait until you get to the end of the path to experience some freedom from suffering. The Buddha taught "the gradual path" (Pāli: anupubbasikkhā). As you progress, you get happier, more contented, more at ease, and you create fewer problems for yourself and others. It is very rewarding when you see your path open in this way. You will have an "Ah-ha!" moment, a situation where something happens, where you act in a more skillful way, and you will think to yourself, "Well, *that* was different!"

The Buddha always tried to teach in a way that would help people to be happier and more skillful and to suffer less. He did this no matter what their situation in life. To that end, he gave advice to husbands and wives, children, rulers of countries, merchants, and people from all walks of life to act more skillfully. He did not limit his teaching just to monks and nuns and lay women and lay men who dedicated their lives to a full awakening.

So that is the first purpose of the practice: to be happier, to be more skillful, to cause less suffering.

However, there is also a super-mundane aspect to the path, and that is final liberation. This aspect of the path can be especially difficult for Westerners to accept, but it is a fundamental part of the Buddha's teachings. He taught that we are reborn, over and over and over, endlessly, and have done so through infinite time. If we live a good, moral life, we improve the chances of having a good rebirth in the human realm or one of the heavenly realms. If we lead a less than moral life, the chances go up that we will be reborn in one of the lower realms, as a (hungry) ghost, an animal, or in one of the hell realms.

This cycle continues until one becomes fully awakened, and a full awakening is the ultimate fruit of the Buddha's path.

How to Practice

The Pāli word for meditation is "bhāvanā." "Bhāvanā" literally means "to develop" or "to cultivate." When you plant a garden, you do not make the seeds grow. You create the optimal conditions for the seeds to grow. The seed will germinate or not based on whether the seed is strong and the conditions are proper, and if it does germinate, that will happen in its own good time. You cannot make a tomato grow overnight.

So you prepare the soil, you plant the seed, you keep it clear of weeds, you water it and feed it, and if everything goes well, after a fashion you will have some tomatoes.

This is very unlike how we are wired in the West. We are results oriented. We want to achieve. We want to be successful. And then we start to meditate, and we get simple instructions, and we can't do them, at least in the beginning. And we get frustrated. We may even quit. All we have done is to find a new way to make ourselves suffer.

The two qualities that will serve you best in meditation are patience and persistence. Persistence is the ability to continue relentlessly, whether or not things appear to be going well. Patience is the ability to have compassion for yourself, and to trust the process, to let it unfold. Accomplished meditators tend to have a lightness about how they deal with problems. They also tend to have a pretty good sense of humor.

There will be parts of your meditation that you find challenging and difficult. This is fine, and one of the things that you learn to do as a meditator is to take those times and not turn them into a problem. So if you have an unpleasant sitting, that is all it is, an unpleasant sitting. You don't have to turn that into a problem.

In fact, one of the important lessons in meditation is how we take non-problems and turn them into problems, take small problems and turn them into big problems, and take bigger problems and turn them into conflagrations. The unawakened mind is a drama queen (or king) at heart.

Meditation is also like exercise. If you exercise skillfully, gradually the weak muscles get stronger. But you must do it, and you must do it skillfully. No one decides to run a marathon one day and runs 26 miles the next day. You start by running however long you can, and over time the distance you can run gets longer.

So it is with meditation. We start with a mind that is likely to be pretty wild. And by working with that mind, every day, as best we can, over time that mind gets stronger, more skillful, and happier.

So the preferred way to practice is to make sure you do it every day and let go of results as best you can. The results will happen if you can do those two things, and it is very gratifying and often a little surprising when the practice manifests.

Summary

1. The purpose of meditation is to reduce and ultimately eliminate suffering for yourself. This has the equal effect of being of benefit to those around you.
2. Meditation requires patience and persistence.
3. Try not to turn your meditation into another problem for yourself.
4. Meditation is like exercise. You must do it regularly to get results. Over time the mind will get stronger, more peaceful, and more discerning.

Establishing a Physical Posture

"Here a [meditator], gone to the forest or to the root of a tree or to an empty hut, sits down; having folded his legs crosswise, set his body erect, and established mindfulness in front of him..."
- [MN 118.17]

It is amazing to me how many long-term meditators still find it difficult to sit comfortably for any length of time. I once went to a retreat at the Bhavana Society where after a few days it was such a problem that one of the senior lay people there offered a workshop on how to sit, and everyone at that retreat had a great deal of experience.

Some meditation teachers will tell you to just somehow grit your teeth and live with whatever pain arises. There will come a time when dealing with physical discomfort will be part of the practice. However, in the beginning it is very important to establish a comfortable sitting posture. In the Tibetan tradition they call this "finding a seat."

There is really only one aim for your physical posture and that is to find a sitting position where you can put the body and leave it there relatively comfortably for the duration of the sitting. If your sitting posture accomplishes that goal, you have found your seat.

However, do not be surprised if it takes some time, effort, and experimentation to find your seat. You may also find that as you age you need to accommodate changes in your body. As with all things in your meditation practice, it requires both patience and persistence to find a rock solid sitting posture.

Establishing a comfortable, stable sitting posture is the first skill that you must master to meditate.

I am going to relegate the instructions on posture to three positions. These do not include any of the lotus positions (full, half, and quarter). They are wonderful postures if you can do them. However, my guess is that if you can do them, you do not need an explanation. This section might be called "postures for the rest of us."

* * *

The Burmese Position

The first posture is sometimes called "the Burmese position." It is a very stable three-point posture that people throughout Asia use, and it is accessible for most people. I have very bad joints and curvature of the spine, and I find this is my most stable position and my preferred posture.

Figure: The Burmese sitting posture

This illustration shows someone on a zafu, which is the traditional meditation cushion, and a zabuton, which is the pad underneath. However, you do not need special cushions for meditation. When I first started I was broke, and I used pillows, blankets, and towels. The Buddha sat on piles of buffalo grass.

As you can see, the knees and feet are on the floor. In all of the postures the hips are tilted forward, and the back is straight. The head should balance on top of the spine, otherwise the shoulders will strain.

Whenever you sit down to meditate, no matter what position you are using, the same principles apply: head, hips, and hands. The head is balanced on top of the spine. You may find it helpful to sway back and forth and side-to-side to find the right balance point. The head is quite heavy. The hips must tilt forward slightly and be open. The hands must not pull the shoulders forward.

The biggest problem with this posture is limited flexibility in the hips. You may feel the strain in the feet or the knees, but the problem is usually in the hips. You may also find that after a longer sitting that the lower back and/or the upper back (shoulders) are strained. It is helpful to know a few stretches to relieve discomfort in these areas. I have a stretching routine that I got from Bob Anderson's book *Stretching*.

In order to keep a good, vertical position and the head balanced, you may find that you have to lean back a bit further than at first feels comfortable. Some people even feel as if they are going to fall over backward. You will have to experiment, but do not be afraid to lean back farther than you think is reasonable.

Another thing that can help in the beginning is when you first sit down, stretch your entire upper body forward and then lean back into a vertical position. Then check that the head balances on top of the spine.

The other issue is the hands. The hands as shown in the photograph are in the preferred position. Some people put their hands on their legs or knees, but this tends to pull the shoulders forward. This creates a lot of strain in the upper back. In order to get your hands at the proper height, you may need to fold your clothing in a way that supports the hands. I have shorter than normal arms so I have to make this adjustment. You can also put a small cushion on your lap to support the hands.

Finally, the dominant hand goes on the bottom, so if you are left-handed, put the left hand on the bottom holding the right hand. If you are right-handed, put the right hand on the bottom holding the left hand.

So the abbreviated summary of bodily posture is this: hips tilted forward, back straight, head balanced on top of the spine, and the hands comfortably on the lap, making sure that they are not pulling the shoulders forward.

The Seiza Position

"Seiza" is the Japanese word for "sitting." In Japan people sit in this position. Unlike Westerners, they do not use cushions or benches. They simply sit on their folded legs. However, as we are not used to it, we usually use a cushion under the buttocks, or a seiza bench:

Figure: The Seiza Position

The instructions for the head, hips, and hands are the same as for the Burmese position.

We are all different heights and have different body proportions. Because of this you have to find the proper spot on the bench on which to sit comfortably. I am short and have found that I need to consciously sit on the front of the bench, otherwise my back and hips are not in the correct position. Someone who is tall will probably need to sit more toward the back of the bench. There are also seiza benches of different heights.

There are many different types of seiza benches, but my experience is that the traditional one works the best. However, do not be afraid to experiment. What works best for me may not work best for you. I also sometimes use a cushion instead of a bench in the seiza position. To do this, just put the cushion between your knees. If the cushion is a zafu, you can turn it on its side. If you are sitting in a Burmese position, it is easy to switch to a seiza position using the cushion. When you are sitting for a long time, such as when you are on retreat, switching back and forth between the Burmese position and the seiza position can make sitting a little more comfortable.

Sitting in a Chair

Most people think that this will be the easiest position, but that is not necessarily true. This is how we ordinarily sit, but we hardly ever sit for very long in a stable posture. You may need to pay a little more attention to how you sit than you normally do.

You want to start by checking the leg position. Chairs are all the same height but people are not. Taller people will find their knees above the hips, and shorter people will find the front of the chair cutting into their upper legs. The idea is to get the upper leg sloping slightly downwards at about a 10-degree angle from the horizontal. Taller people may need to put cushions under the buttocks; shorter people will need to put cushions or towels or blankets under their feet.

Sit on the forward part of the chair. Do not lean against the back of the chair. Put the head, hips, and hands in the same position as described for the Burmese position. I find the hardest part is keeping the hips cocked forward and the back straight. A cushion may help to keep the hips leaning forward properly.

One chair that works well for me is the "tilt seat eco chair" made by Carolina Designs. I tried many of the so-called ergonomic chairs without any success, but this one works well for me.

A few years ago I had a knee injury and could not sit on the floor, so I bought one of these. I also bought a cushion for it, which is a separate item.

Figure: The Tilt Seat

However, I realize that not everyone will want to buy a special chair. Be assured that by using towels and pillows and whatever you have available, you can make a chair work. Stick to the principles of head, hips and hands and maintaining the proper angle at the knees.

How Long to Meditate

It takes a while to establish a stable and comfortable position. Just like running a marathon, do not over-do it in the beginning. Find a length of time that works for you. I started with five minutes. That seemed like an eternity. Work your way up slowly. You may add a minute a day, or five minutes a week. Do whatever makes you feel comfortable, and then sit just a while longer.

The standard sitting times are 45 minutes or an hour. However, I find that as little as 10 minutes is enough to establish a calmer, more settled state of mind. 20 minutes is better. You will have to find some time that fits into your daily schedule. Try to make this somewhere between 20 minutes and an hour. However, as I said, in the beginning start with what you can do, perhaps just five minutes, and work your way up.

We will also be doing a practice shortly called "sweeping" that is helpful in establishing a comfortable posture.

You can use any convenient timer. It is good to use a timer and not a watch. If you are using a watch you have to keep looking at it, which is a distraction. For a long time I just used a kitchen timer. Then I switched to a "GymBoss timer." Now I use an iPad application. But anything that keeps you from having to look at a watch is fine.

There is one last thing. Despite what I said about being comfortable, one of the things we are trying to learn is how to work with discomfort. We want to make it workable. No matter how much we may want life to be a certain way, it has a habit of being just the way it is. This includes mental and physical discomfort. In meditation, we are not trying to make those go away. They won't anyway, so there is no point to it. We are trying to not make the discomfort into a problem. Thus, if you feel a little discomfort, do not quickly respond by shifting or changing position. Sit with it a little and see what happens. See if it goes away. See if it changes. Get to know it. That is "making it workable."

I have a "three strikes and you are out" rule. The first time I feel something unpleasant, I just sit with it and see what happens. It will usually go away. Then I do this a second time. By the third time I feel it, I will usually change position, slowly and mindfully.

There will come a time when the discomfort fades into the background. I heard a story once about a young man who entered a Zen monastery in Japan. He really had trouble with sitting, and in Zen monasteries they are very strict about not moving during a sitting. He had a lot of pain. Finally he gave up and decided to quit the monastery. When he was having his exit interview with the abbot he asked, "If I were to stay here another six months, would the pain go away?" "No," replied the abbot, "But you wouldn't care anymore."

The way I am going to teach meditation will - I hope - not cause you this kind of pain. The moral of the story is that at some point your concentration will be such that any discomfort you feel will not matter anymore. This is a great lesson in the power of the mind and the practice.

Summary

This is a lengthy discussion here of how to do something that we do every day. But it is an example of how little we know about our bodies. You have already learned a great deal that most people do not know. Getting to know the body is one of the most important aspects of meditation practice. It is so important that the "Kāyagatāsati Sutta: Mindfulness of the Body" [MN 119] describes an entire path to final liberation using only the body as the object of meditation.

1. The goal of your sitting posture is to find a position where you can put the body and leave it there relatively comfortably for the duration of the sitting.
2. Regardless of the position, the same principles apply: head, hips, and hands. The head balances on top of the spine. The hips tilt forward and are open. The hands must not pull the shoulders forward.
3. If you are sitting on a chair, make sure that the knees are at the proper angle.
4. Use a timer and not a watch so you can meditate without being distracted.

Establishing a Mental Posture

At Sāvatthī. Standing to one side, that devatā recited this verse in the presence of the Blessed One:

"Those who dwell deep in the forest,
Peaceful, leading the holy life,
Eating but a single meal a day,
Why are their faces
so bright and serene?"

[The Blessed One:]
"They do not sorrow over the past,
don't long for the future.
They survive on the present,
That's why their faces
are bright and serene."

"From longing for the future,
From sorrowing over the past,
fools wither away
Like a green reed cut down."
- [SN 1.10]

Once you establish a physical posture, the next step is to establish a mental posture. This means leaving behind all of your distracted thoughts, your preoccupations, thinking about the past, worrying about the future, and bringing your mind completely into the present moment.

The process that I describe here is one that I learned some years ago at a meditation retreat. I still use it, and there is a certain comfort – a feeling of coming home – that you can get by having a set routine every time that you sit down to meditate. This process has five steps:

1. Gratitude
2. Remembering why we practice
3. Loving-kindness for yourself
4. The five subjects for frequent recollection
5. Turning your attention to the breath

Gratitude

I am grateful for what I am and have. My thanksgiving is perpetual.

- [Henry David Thoreau, *Familiar Letters of Henry David Thoreau*]

Start by sitting on the cushion or chair, checking your head, hips, and hands, getting the body into a position where you can leave it for the duration of the sitting, and then take several deep breaths. As you inhale feel the breath energy spread to the whole body. As you exhale, release any tension you have in the body and in the mind. Bring your body and mind to as calm a state as you can.

Then we want to establish a feeling of gratitude.

The Buddha said this about gratitude:

"...one possessing four qualities is deposited in heaven as if brought there. What four? Bodily good conduct, verbal good conduct, mental good conduct, and gratitude or thankfulness. One possessing these four qualities is deposited in heaven as if brought there."
- [AN 4.213]

You can establish gratitude in any way that works for you. You may feel gratitude for a friend, parent, child, situation, the gift of having a human life. It can be anything. You can feel gratitude simply for the opportunity to learn meditation. This is a "worldly way" to establish a mind of gratitude.

Traditionally in Buddhism you establish gratitude for the Three Jewels: the Buddha, the Dharma, and the Saṇgha. The Buddha is the person without whom we would not have these teachings. He gave up a life of wealth, ease, and comfort, and at great sacrifice he discovered the path to awakening.

The word "Dharma" has several meanings, but in this case Dharma means the teachings of the Buddha, the understanding of how life works. The Buddha left an enormous number of discourses numbering many thousands of pages that describe our state in life and how to improve it. It is a gift of immeasurable value.

The word "saṇgha" literally means "community." In modern times it has come to mean anyone in the Buddhist community. However, traditionally there were two types of Saṇgha. One is the "monastic Saṇgha," the community of monks and nuns. These are the people who give up traditional pleasures to devote themselves full-time to this practice. They are also the ones who preserve the tradition and embody it.

The second type of Saṇgha is the "noble Saṇgha." These are the people who have attained an awakening, people who are enlightened. Because there are lay people who are enlightened, the noble Saṇgha is not a subset of the monastic Saṇgha. The noble Saṇgha is especially inspirational to those who seek awakening. They show it can be done; they are a model for our own aspirations.

Feeling gratitude for the Buddha, the Dharma, and the Saṇgha is a transcendent way to establish gratitude. That is not to make the worldly way somehow inferior. Whatever works for you is fine. Sit with this feeling for a few moments, whatever feels comfortable for you.

Remember Why We Are Practicing

The next step is to remember why we are practicing. It is so easy to sit down and start to watch the breath and not remember why we are bothering to do this in the first place.

"...there are these four kinds of persons found existing in the world. What four? One who is practicing neither for his own welfare nor for the welfare of others; one who is practicing for the welfare of others but not for his own welfare; one who is practicing for his own welfare but not for the welfare of others; and one who is practicing both for his own welfare and for the welfare of others.

"...The person practicing both for his own welfare and for the welfare of others is the foremost, the best, the preeminent, the supreme, and the finest of these four persons."
- [AN 4.95]

We are not just sitting here watching the breath to kill time. This is important business. At stake is our own happiness and peace of mind. And as we become more skillful, we are of great benefit to those around us. These two things are inextricably linked. We practice to become happy and useful. This step is to bring those two purposes into the forefront.

Loving-kindness

The next step is to establish a mind of loving-kindness and good will for yourself. The Pāli word is "mettā." It literally means "love," but the word "love" is so emotionally charged and abused that "mettā" is usually translated as "loving-kindness."

It is important to have respect for yourself, especially in this practice. The mere fact that you are reading this makes you an unusual person, someone with a good heart and wise intentions. You should have respect for that. You should love yourself as much or more than anyone else in your life. You must be your own best friend.

There is this story from the Pāli Canon. King Pasenadi was the King of Kosala, one of the two superpowers in ancient India. Queen Mallikā had been a poor girl who King Pasenadi made his queen:

I have heard that on one occasion the [Buddha] was staying near Sāvatthī at Jeta's Grove, Anāthapiṇḍika's monastery. And on that occasion King Pasenadi had gone with Queen Mallikā to the upper palace. Then he said to her, "Mallikā, is there anyone dearer to you than yourself?"

"No, great King. There is no one dearer to me than myself. And what about you, great King? Is there anyone dearer to you than yourself?"

"No, Mallikā. There is no one dearer to me than myself."

Then the King, descending from the palace, went to the Blessed One and, on arrival, having bowed down to him, sat to one side. As he was sitting there, he said to the Blessed One, "Just now, when I had gone with Queen Mallikā to the upper palace, I said to her, 'Mallikā, is there anyone dearer to you than yourself?'

"When this was said, she said to me, 'No, great King. There is no one dearer to me than myself. And what about you, great King? Is there anyone dearer to you than yourself?'

"When this was said, I said to her, 'No, Mallikā. There is no one dearer to me than myself.'"

Then, on realizing the significance of that, the [Buddha] on that occasion exclaimed:

> *"Searching all directions*
> *with your awareness,*
> *you find no one dearer*

than yourself.
In the same way, others
are thickly dear to themselves.
So you shouldn't hurt others
if you love yourself."
- [Ud 5.1]

This, of course, is not narcissistic love. It is a genuine wish for your own happiness and well-being.

One way to establish mettā for yourself is to think of someone who you love dearly, someone for whom you wish nothing but happiness. Babies and children are good objects of mettā. Our agendas for them are more pure and more altruistic. Once you have established that feeling for them, you can turn that feeling onto yourself. Another technique that is helpful is to think of yourself as a baby, and think how much you would love and care for that baby.

Five Subjects for Frequent Recollection

The next step is remembering the five subjects for frequent recollection. There is a discourse by this name chanted daily in monasteries around the world.

The five subjects are:

1. We are all subject to sickness.
2. We are all subject to aging.
3. We are all subject to death.
4. Everything that we know and love we will leave behind.
5. The one thing that we take with us is our karma, the fruits of our actions, both good and bad.

The intention here is to conjure up a sense of urgency and to keep us focused on the prize. What matters most in our lives is the basic goodness that we develop. We do this on and off of the cushion, and they reinforce each other.

Turn Your Attention to the Breath

Once you have reviewed the five subjects, it is time to turn your attention to the breath. In the next chapter we will discuss the topic of breath meditation. For now it is enough to understand that in the beginning we just want to know the breath.

There is a very poetic passage from the Pāli Canon about this step in the meditation process. You may want to memorize it, and use it as the entry point to watching the breath:

"And how does a [meditator] abide contemplating the body as a body? Here a [meditator], having gone to the forest or to the root of a tree or to an empty hut, sits down; folds her legs crosswise, sets her body erect, and establishes mindfulness in front of her, ever mindful she breathes in, mindful she breathes out."
- [MN 10.4]

Summary

In order to establish a mental posture, perform the following steps:

1. Take several deep, cleansing breaths.
2. Establish gratitude in the mind.
3. Remember why you are practicing.
4. Establish loving-kindness for yourself.
5. Remember the five subjects for frequent recollection.
6. Turn your attention to the breath.

* * *

"— on that occasion a [meditator] abides contemplating the body as a body, ardent, fully aware, and mindful, having put away covetousness and grief for the world."

- [MN 118.24]

Breath Meditation

"Bhikkhus, when mindfulness of breathing is developed and cultivated, it is of great fruit and great benefit. When mindfulness of breathing is developed and cultivated, it fulfills the four foundations of mindfulness. When the four foundations of mindfulness are developed and cultivated, they fulfill the seven enlightenment factors. When the seven enlightenment factors are developed and cultivated, they fulfill true knowledge and deliverance."
- [MN 118.15]

Once you have established both a physical posture and a mental posture, the next step is to turn your attention to the breath.

There are many objects of meditation. The commentarial work *The Visuddhimagga* lists 40 such objects. However, from the time of the Buddha the breath has been the most used and most common object of meditation. The Buddha's most complete instructions on meditation are in the "Ānāpānasati Sutta: Mindfulness of Breathing" [MN 118].

The Buddha never gave specific instructions on where in the body to do this. And in future lessons we will discuss various places to follow the breath. But for now, start by following it at the nostrils. There you can feel the air moving in and out of the body.

Some years ago I went to a retreat with the Viet Namese monk Thich Nhat Hanh where he said that in all the decades in which he had done breath meditation, the breath had always been fascinating, and it had never become boring. At the time, frankly, I could not imagine that. But as the years have gone by, I have seen that what the breath reveals is almost infinite.

The first thing to do in following the breath at the nostrils is to find the places where the breath is felt most strongly. This may be at the tips of the nostrils, farther up in the nose, just below the nose, at the upper lip, etc. You may feel it at one place on the in-breath and another on the out-breath. And at different sittings, you may feel it at different spots. So start every sitting by finding the precise location where you feel the breath most strongly.

As you do this, you may notice that a single breath can be broken into parts. Before the next in-breath there is often a pause, a still moment when the breath is not moving in or out. Then you begin the in-breath. The breath at this point may feel very faint. Next, you move into the middle part of the breath, and the end of the in-breath follows that.

Some people feel a slight pause between the in-breath and the out-breath. Then the out-breath, likewise, has a beginning, a middle, and an end.

In order to see these parts, you must follow the breath all the way in and all the way out. This is the fundamental way to do breath meditation.

Expanding the Awareness

As the mind and body get more settled, you may find your awareness naturally expanding to fill the whole body. This is the desired result. If you do not experience this at this point, that is fine. Do not worry about. But at some point you will probably feel this happening. It is an expanded sense of awareness.

This expanded sense of awareness is very important in breath meditation, and it is what the Buddha himself taught. In the Ānāpānasati Sutta, the first three steps are given as follows:

"Breathing in long, [the meditator] discerns, 'I am breathing in long'; or breathing out long, he discerns, 'I am breathing out long.' Or breathing in short, he discerns, 'I am breathing in short'; or breathing out short, he discerns, 'I am breathing out short.' He trains himself, 'I will breathe in sensitive to the entire body.' He trains himself, 'I will breathe out sensitive to the entire body.'"
- [MN 118.18]

What I am calling "the breath" is really "breath energy." As you breathe in and out, you may feel the breath energy anywhere in the body. You may want to play with this a little to confirm what I am saying. Put your attention somewhere else for a few breaths. It could be anywhere: the hands, the center of the chest, the throat, the soles of the feet. You can sense breathing in and breathing out anywhere in the body.

This introduces a couple of very important topics. The first is playing with the breath. Meditation is about learning. Larry Rosenberg says that in Buddhist meditation, we learn our way out of suffering. Here we are beginning to learn about our bodies and the breath. You may have heard the instruction to simply be with the breath. That is one way to meditate, and it can be quite wonderful. But that type of practice is very difficult to do in the beginning. Most of the Buddha's instructions are, in fact, what I call "active meditation." This means that you are not simply observing what is going on. You are doing something with the breath.

The other important topic is how you can feel the breath anywhere in the body. A further refinement is to play with different types of breathing to see what effect they have. You can breathe short on the in-breath and long on the out-breath. You can reverse that. You can breathe short on both the in-breath and the out-breath, and conversely, breathe long on the in-breath and the out-breath. This begins to give you a sense of the range of experience you can have using the breath. It becomes an active part of your meditative toolbox. You get to know the effects of different kinds of breathing, and you can use them as necessary. When the mind is dull, apply the appropriate breath antidote. When the mind is restless, likewise. This is how you begin to make the mind workable.

Most of us live our lives at the mercy of our habits and conditioning. They are in control. Meditation is a way to train the mind in order for us to get that control back. Usually our thoughts and emotions are in charge.

The way I described allowing the attention to expand to fill the whole body is a passive way to do this. You just let it happen naturally. However, you can also try to do this actively. Take your attention on the breath and expand it to fill the body. If this does not work for you at this point, do not worry about it. Just know that this is possible.

Finally, on the out-breath, try to breathe out through the entire body. It is as if the physical body is inside a cocoon of energy. As with all of these practices, if you cannot feel this in the beginning, do not worry about it. Just breathe in whatever way you find pleasant. But know that eventually this feeling of bodily breath energy may actually become stronger than your feeling of the physical body. The sense of the physical body will fade into the background, and the sense of the "breath-body" will become strong.

Coming Back to the Breath

Inevitably your attention will wander. We have a lifetime of experience doing that, and in the modern world we have raised the quality of distraction to high art. Reversing that trend will take time.

When you see that your mind has wandered off of the breath, the first thing to do is see this is a good thing. It is a moment of awareness. This is one of the things we are trying to cultivate. Most people never have a moment like this. Congratulate yourself.

Next you want to bring your attention back to the breath. How you do this is extremely important. You want to take several pleasant breaths. Breathe in a way that feels good.

Ajahn Brahm, who is the abbot of Bodhinyana monastery in Australia, uses the term the "beautiful breath." What constitutes the beautiful breath depends on the circumstances. If you are feeling a lot of stress, the beautiful breath may be very deep and long. In other circumstances, it may be short, or short in and long out. This is part of the skill of meditation. You are developing skills. But you have to be the one who knows how and when to use these skills. Meditation is a uniquely personal thing.

There is both an art and a craft to meditation. If you take 20 gifted young artists, and you put them into an art school, and they all take the same courses, still no two of them will produce the same art. You are learning skills, getting to know the mind, and putting some tools in your meditative toolbox. That is the craft of meditation. However, eventually you will become an artist. That is when your unique path in meditation will become very personal, and that will start to happen very early in the process.

Quieting the Mind

The final step in these instructions is to quiet the mind. This is not easy. A great deal of meditation time is spent trying to quiet the mind.

A mind that is always racing about is not a very good instrument. In order to see the things that we need to see, the mind must be quiet.

Ṭhānissaro Bhikkhu says that quieting the mind is like going into a house where the refrigerator is running. When it stops running, suddenly you hear all the other noises that you could not hear before. In order to see the subtle things that we need to see, we need to get the mind to settle down.

Serenity, tranquility, and calm also have many other benefits. We are less reactive. We are less self-centered. We begin to connect more with people. We are more compassionate and understanding. We have less anxiety, anger, and fear. We crave less. We are more at peace with the world. We are more at peace with ourselves. The quiet mind is wiser and more skillful. The benefits are almost endless.

In the next chapter I will describe other methods for getting the mind more concentrated. However, everything that follows is an expansion of what is here. We start by focusing our attention on a single spot, which at this stage is the nose. Then we expand our awareness to the whole body. Then we expand it still further to the mind, to get it quieter. These three things are kept in balance. In the first phase of meditation training, this is the objective.

Watching Your Thoughts

I will give you one other thing to play with here. You may not be able to see this at first, but you can actually watch your thoughts. Normally in breath meditation, most – but not all – of your attention is on the breath. The rest of your attention – your background attention – focuses on everything else. This background attention is always present. It is why you can be doing one thing and suddenly see something else, like a car driving by.

Larry Rosenberg uses the 80-20 rule; 80% of your attention is on the breath, and 20% is on everything else.

However, you can also reverse that percentage and put 20% of your attention on the breath and 80% on something else. This is one of the fundamental principles in "ānāpānasati," mindfulness of breathing. We start by making the breath the object of meditation. Then we use the breath as a way to stabilize the mind, to give it a kind of rhythm, a heartbeat. We use that heartbeat to look at other things. In this case, we have already done that by expanding our awareness to the whole body.

In the case of our thoughts, we put 20% of the attention on the breath and the other 80% on our minds. Then you can see thoughts actually forming. Like everything else in life they have a beginning, a middle, and an end. One of the things you can use this type of meditation for is to quiet the mind. Sometimes by watching the thoughts, they will go away.

What usually happens when you think is that one thought arises, and this begins a proliferation of thoughts. You are watching the breath and a thought arises, and suddenly your attention to the breath is lost. You are chasing a thought stream. You get lost in a world that exists only in your mind.

Watching your thoughts has almost endless possibilities. You can see where in the mind a thought arises. You can catch the thought so it does not proliferate. Even more subtly you can stop it dead in its racks. You can actually keep it from finishing. It is a fascinating process.

You have probably guessed that this is not easy. However, I introduce it here as another way to get the mind a little quieter. If focusing on the breath is not working, you may try simply watching your thoughts.

Dedication of Merit

"Bhikkhus, there are these three bases of meritorious activity. What three? The basis of meritorious activity consisting in giving; the basis of meritorious activity consisting in virtuous behavior; and the basis of meritorious activity consisting in meditative development."
- [AN 8.36]

One of the traditions in Buddhism is making merit. As you can see from the Buddha's words, this is done in three ways: generosity, virtue, and the practice of meditation. Every time that you meditate, you are making merit for yourself and others. It is another way of saying that you are creating good karma.

It is customary at the end of a meditation session to dedicate the merit of your effort to all beings. The effort that goes into meditation is not just for you; it is for the health and well-being of everyone.

There are a number of ways of dedicating merit. At the Abhayagiri Monastery in California, they chant the "Reflection on Sharing Blessings." You can also simply recite these words:

May the merit of this effort be shared by all beings, so that they may be liberated.

This brings us full circle to when we established a mental posture and remembered why we practice. It is for our own happiness and for the happiness of all beings.

In addition, you may dedicate the merit of your meditation to a specific person. This person may be alive or dead. You can do this for someone who is going through a difficult time or someone who died to whom you want to send positive karmic energy. You can do this in any way that you like, something like:

May the merit of this effort be dedicated to [someone], so that they may find peace and harmony.

The words can be whatever you want.

Finally, as you get up from your meditation, stay in touch with the breath. Do this throughout the day. Keep coming back to the breath as a way of connecting to the present moment. And also keep the good spirit in your heart that comes from the dedication of merit. By meditating you are doing a noble act with a noble intention.

Summary

This chapter introduces the fundamental approach to breath meditation:

1. Find a spot on which to focus and watch the breath coming in and out.
2. Passively or actively expand the attention to include the whole body.
3. When the mind wanders, bring your attention back to the breath by breathing in a way that feels good.
4. When you feel it is possible, further expand your awareness to include the mind to get the mind to settle down.
5. Try watching your thoughts as a way to quiet the mind.
6. When your meditation period ends, dedicate the merit of your effort to all beings.

More Meditation Techniques

From what I've observed in my own practice, there is only one path that is short, easy, effective and pleasant, and at the same time has hardly anything to lead you astray: the path of keeping the breath in mind, the same path the Lord Buddha himself used with such good results.

- [Ajahn Lee Dhammadharo, *Keeping the Breath in Mind*]

The instructions given in the previous chapter are probably enough to keep you going for a very long time, perhaps, as Thich Nhat Hanh noted, many decades. To be sure, we will be going into some detail on what breath meditation reveals, and we will be expanding the use of the breath to investigate other topics of meditation.

The instructions just given are relatively simple. But just because something is simple, that does not mean it is easy. In baseball, pitchers spend their entire careers trying to throw the same pitches over and over, and batters try to perfect the art of hitting those pitches. Conceptually both actions are easy to understand and easy to explain. They are, however, extremely difficult to do consistently.

So over the centuries many techniques were developed to cultivate a stable, concentrated, tranquil mind. A few of them are described here.

There are an almost infinite number of meditation techniques. This points to how hard it is to fully develop concentration. You should feel free to experiment. Just keep in mind that the goal at this point is to a) develop a broad-based form of concentration and b) to quiet the mind. If the meditation technique that you choose does not satisfy these criteria it will be counterproductive.

Another Beautiful Breath

This first technique is quite simple, but satisfies the criteria for being a "beautiful breath." It combines both active and passive breath meditation.

In order to do this type of meditation you must be able to experience whole body awareness. You must be able to feel the breath energy expand to fill the whole body.

In this technique, when you breathe in take control of the breath and breathe in until the breath energy expands to fill the whole body. You will have to play with the breath to feel when the breath energy is full enough but not too full. One way to do this is to "bracket," that is, intentionally breath in too deeply and, conversely, breath in a way that is clearly too shallow. The correct level of breathing will be in between. It should feel good.

Now when you begin to breathe out, simply let go of any control of the breath and let the breath exhale naturally. It is like sliding down a playground slide. Now you just watch the breath and feel it as it goes out naturally. It should come to a nice, calm, quiet conclusion. In Zen they call this "letting go into silence."

This type of breathing is especially soothing and satisfying. It is also a good introduction to simply letting the breath be.

Breath Counting

The next meditation technique is breath counting. When I started to meditate I was in a Zen group, and this is what they taught me. I still find it useful.

There are many ways to count the breaths. The first way is to count once at the beginning of the in-breath and once again on the out-breath. If you are new to meditation, this is the place to start.

The next way to count breaths is to either just count on the in-breath or the out-breath. Try both to see which works best for you.

If you can see your thoughts, try this experiment. See whether your thoughts tend to begin on the in-breath or the out-breath or both. If one is dominant, count those breaths. My thoughts tend to start on the in-breath, so counting in-breaths works best for me. But see how it is for you, and see which method of counting helps get your mind settled, and which one helps you concentrate better.

See if you can get to a point where you can count just the in-breath or the out-breath, ten breaths, three times in a row. When I started, it took me several months to get to this point. It takes time.

Once you can consistently get to 30, switch to using just a single word, like "in" on the in-breath and "out" on the out-breath. In Thailand, they use the word "buddho," which means "awake." They say (silently) "bud" on the in-breath and "dho" on the out-breath.

When you can use "in-out" or "buddho" consistently, you can drop the noting word and simply follow the breath.

One way to combine these is to use a countdown timer that repeats. Set it to four iterations of five minutes each. For the first five minutes, count both the in-breath and the out-breath. For the next five minutes, count just the in-breath or the out-breath. For the next five minutes, use a noting word, and for the last five minutes, just follow the breath.

You can do breath counting or use a noting word off of the cushion as well. Put 20% of your attention on the breath and start counting or noting. This can be done while walking, driving, etc., and can be a pleasant way to calm down and be more in the present moment. If you are driving, of course, make sure that you pay proper attention to that. The world needs all the meditators it can get.

Sweeping

Sweeping is one of my favorite practices. It can have several different purposes. Here we are using it to develop tranquility and concentration.

There are many different ways to do sweeping. This approach is the one that I have come to favor after many years of trying various techniques. It emphasizes the energy centers and flows in the body, particularly the chakras. However, there are other ways to do it, and as usual you should feel free to try others. But this is the one that I think gives optimal results.

Before I describe sweeping, it is useful for you to know something about the chakras. Chakras are energy centers in the body. Just as the body as a whole is energy, within the whole-body energy system, there are places were the energy is stronger. Each center has different qualities associated with it. The major chakras are the top of the head, the forehead, the throat, the center of the chest, the base of the sternum, the abdomen, and the base of the spine.

There are also minor chakras. There are two in particular that are very helpful in breath meditation. Those are in the palms of the hands and the soles of the feet. However, as you work with the body, you may find energy centers almost anywhere. The Thai Forest Monk Ajahn Lee had a strong energy center at the base of the neck.

This is part of the fun of meditation, this process of discovery. You are getting to know your body in an intimate way. And it is not static. It may and will be different on different days.

Figure: The Major Chakras

Conversely, you will have more trouble feeling the breath energy in other areas. Joints can act like closed valves that prevent the breath energy from flowing into the extremities. Energy tends to flow along the long bones, but the energy may not flow along one or more of them. Simply try to get the breath energy flowing. Work on an area until the effort is not producing any result, and then move on to the next spot.

If it is not clear already, in breath meditation, you start by picking one spot through which to follow the breath energy. You can do this for as long as you like. You want to establish yourself at that point.

If this proves to be a problem, one option is to change the point at which you are following the breath. You can follow it pretty much anywhere in the body. Try moving the point up or down in the body and see what that does. If you are having trouble maintaining focus at the nose, for example, try moving it down into the abdomen, or all the way down to the soles of the feet. The chakras are good places to try.

An alternative is to pick two or three different spots at which to follow the breath. This can work well because you have to balance your attention across multiple spots. It forces you to use more energy. It also facilitates the flow of bodily energies. These can be any spots you want. For example, you can use the nose, the palms of the hands, and the soles of the feet.

When doing spot meditation, you usually breathe in and out through that spot or spots. An alternative is to breathe in through the primary spot or spots, and then out through another spot. For example, you can breathe in though the soles of the feet, and out through the crown chakra. This draws the energy up from the feet, through the whole body, and out through the top of the head. You can go the other way as well.

Once you can establish focus in this way, your attention will either expand naturally to fill the whole body, or you can try and make that happen. In time you will be able to do these two basic steps – starting with one or more points and then expanding to the whole body – easily. If you expand to the whole body and then have trouble maintaining focus, go back to your original spot(s).

Once you expand your awareness to the whole body, when you breathe out, you want to breathe out through the whole body. You want to breathe out into the air. You may have a sense of the bodily energy diffusing into the surrounding air. This can be incredibly soothing and relaxing.

When the attention wanders, when you catch yourself, breathe in and out for several breaths in a particularly beautiful way. It should feel good.

When you are doing the sweeping practice, you work with each spot in the same way. The difference is that rather than picking a spot or spots with which to work, you will work through the body in a systematic way. When you have done a lot of this more structured work, you will get a feel for how different types of breathing work for you. This is a great advantage, especially for less experienced meditators. It won't tell you all the possibilities for how to work with the breath – which is almost endless – but you will begin to get a sense of how the energies feel to you in your body, and how they work for you.

The next step is to understand when to use which technique. Suppose you have tension at the temples. This usually means that you want to draw the energy down. You can switch to the abdomen or the soles of the feet. Or you can breathe out through the whole head, drawing the tension out. Or you can start at the temples and draw the energy of the in-breath to another spot, like the base of the spine.

There are no fixed rules. Treat it as an experiment. Try something for a few minutes and see what the results are. Be patient, and give each strategy a chance. Most people eventually develop a set of strategies that works for them. It is uniquely personal. Everyone will experience things differently.

Some people criticize this as being too concerned with technique. It can be, and you want to watch out for that. But this is a skill. Compare it to baseball. Hitters and pitchers and fielders make adjustments on almost every pitch depending on the situation. If a hitter has two strikes on him/her, he/she may choke up on the bat, protect the plate, and try to hit the ball to the opposite field. Fielders may shade toward the opposite field to guard against that. If there are less than three balls, the pitcher may try to throw it out of the strike zone and get the batter to chase a bad pitch. That is just one situation, and it does not take into account the inning, score, runners on base, the number of outs, or the skills of the players involved. They make constant and often subtle adjustments.

This is the skill of meditation. It takes years and years and years for great athletes to become skilled baseball players. It is the same way with meditation. And things always change. Your life situation will change. Sometimes you will be healthy, at other times not. You will age. You will move, change jobs, go in and out of relationships.

This is why sweeping can be such an effective practice. It slows things down. If you are having a problem, you can walk your way systematically through the body and see what makes a difference and in what way. You may have been meditating for years and years, but then something changes. Sweeping gets you back to a place where you can hit the meditational reset button. But also remember that you can breathe in and out in so many different ways. This type of sweeping meditation gives you a taste of the possibilities, but it is just a taste.

For this type of sweeping, start by using the abdomen as your primary center of attention. Breathe in through the abdomen, expanding your awareness to the whole body, then either breathe out through the whole body, or back out through the abdomen.

Then start moving your way up, to the solar plexus, the heart center, and the base of the throat. Take your time.

Then move your attention into the center of the head. Breathe in through all of the openings: the nose, the eyes, and the ears. Breathe out through the whole head. Look for any tension, especially in the joints of the jaw and the temples. Try and get everything relaxed.

If you have a lot of attention in the upper body or the head, you can try breathing out through the soles of the feet, or possibly the abdomen, somewhere lower in the body.

Remember always that we are trying to establish a feeling of comfort and ease. It is very natural to actually tense up while you are trying to relax. Something doesn't work, so you "try harder," and this just makes things worse. If the tension gets too pronounced, try just taking some nice, deep breaths, filling the whole body with ease.

When working with the head, you can also use the chakras there. One of them is in the forehead. This is the "mind's eye," "Dhamma eye," or "third eye." You can breathe in through the third eye, through the head, and all the way down and out the soles of the feet. This is just a suggestion. You can breathe in and out however and wherever you want.

The other chakra in the head is at the crown of the head. The crown chakra is quite interesting. It is associated with consciousness itself. The Tibetans have a practice of "conscious dying" in which they work with getting the consciousness to leave the body through the crown chakra. Work with it and see how it feels to you. You may feel a slight tingling.

Once you make your way into the head, you have experienced most of the major chakras. You may experience the chakras in different ways. Some people feel them as energy centers. I think this is quite common. (That is actually what they are.) You may also feel a swirling pool of energy, like water going down a drain. Some people experience the chakras as light. Each chakra has a different color associated with it:

1. The root chakra (base of the spine) is red.
2. The sacral chakra (just below the belly button) is orange.
3. The solar plexus chakra is yellow.
4. The heart chakra is green.
5. The throat chakra is blue.
6. The third eye is indigo.
7. The crown chakra is either purple or white.

This may – will – take time. In meditation, you never know when something will happen. You may struggle for months just to work your way through the body, then one day you will feel a strong energy somewhere, or maybe that whirlpool of energy or a bright light. When this happens, you will probably be startled and will pull back. That is fine and completely normal. Over time, you will get used to it, and it will work its way into your comfort zone. You will enjoy it. There is a feeling of empowerment as you gain mastery over this disorderly mind.

Once you are as settled as you can get in the head, move your attention to the base of the neck. On the in-breath, breathe down the arms and out the fingers. You may feel beams of energy going out of the fingers. On the out-breath, breathe out through the arms. Let the energy dissipate into the surrounding air.

When the neck and arms feel as settled as you can get them, breathe from the base of the neck and down both sides of the spine down to the base of the spine. The base of the spine is the final major chakra. Breathe out from the spine into the surrounding air.

Once you have worked the spine to your satisfaction, move your attention to the base of the spine. On the in-breath, breathe down through the legs and out the toes. As with the fingers, you may feel beams of energy flowing out of the toes. On the out-breath, breathe out through the legs into the surrounding air.

This completes one sweep of the body.

There is quite a lot here with which to work. Take your time, as always. Be patient, and be kind to yourself. Let it unfold. Plant your seeds. Water the ground. Pull the weeds. The seeds will sprout when they are ready.

Sweeping is especially good at fostering a broad sense of awareness. At a certain point when you breathe in, the breath energy will flow to fill the whole body. Sweeping is a way of breaking the body down into energy channels. Eventually, you will be able to put all the pieces back together. You will feel the whole body on the in-breath and the whole body on the out-breath. That is what we are after. There will be some days where the energy flows freely as soon as you start to do breath meditation. On other days it will not flow as well. This is an indication that sweeping may help you.

You can do this sweeping practice for as long as it is useful. I heard about a retreat where all they did for the first six months was sweeping. You can make this your main practice. Once you feel it no longer has value, you can use it as necessary, such as on days when the breath energy is not flowing freely. You can also do it just for fun. It is a very soothing practice, and there is nothing wrong with doing something just because it's fun. This is the "pleasure born of seclusion." There is no danger in this type of pleasure. It is very pleasant, and it was a fundamental part of his journey to enlightenment.

Many people think that meditation is dull, hard, serious work. That is contrary to what we are trying to do here. The objective is to develop a state of mind that has joy and happiness as its primary traits. It is hard to do that if you are feeling grumpy. The purpose of the entire first stage of training is to establish a sense of well-being, a place of safety and comfort. It is your home base. If you never do anything in your meditation practice but that, you will be better off than almost everyone else on the planet.

There is a very good guided meditation on the Internet for this type of sweeping meditation. You can find it by searching for "youtube chakra sweeping meditation."

Summary

We have added a number of useful breath meditation techniques:

1. A new type of breathing practice
2. Breath counting and noting
3. Body sweeping

Problems While Meditating

Everyone encounters problems and difficult patches in the course of meditating, so don't let them get you upset. Don't view them as signs that you're making no progress or that you're a hopeless meditator. Problems are an excellent opportunity for figuring out where you have unskillful habits and learning how to do something about them. This is what develops your discernment. In fact, the process of learning how to deal with the two most common problems in meditation, pain and wandering thoughts, is what has brought many people in the past to awakening.

- [Ṭhānissaro Bhikkhu, *With Each & Every Breath*]

The mind is a complex thing, and when you meditate a myriad of problems come up. I can't cover every possible contingency, so I am going to address the most common issues. The most important principle to remember is that at this stage in your meditation practice, the goal is to cultivate concentration and tranquility. Any activity or meditation practice that aids that process is helpful. Anything else is not.

There will come a time when turning your attention towards a painful mind state will be the practice. Many teachers tell you to do it at this point, at an early stage of your practice. You can do that now, but it is an extremely challenging and painful way to proceed. What we are trying to do is to lay a groundwork of well-being so that those difficult mind states become more workable.

Breathing Through the Distraction

The most common problem is simply staying with the breath. There are two methods that I find work in most cases. The first one is breathing through the problem. Put yourself in a frame of mind where you are keeping most of your attention on the breath and some of your attention on your thoughts (i.e., the 80-20 rule). When you see a thought begin to arise, breathe right through it.

Another category of problems is when there is a personal issue that is very strong. This may be a powerful emotion – like fear – or a problem like death, illness, divorce, a lost job. See if you can breathe through those thoughts as well.

Apropos of difficult life issues, I have already mentioned the practice of mettā, loving-kindness. Later we will discuss a more formal way to do this. For now, if you are in a difficult life situation, it is helpful to know that part of mettā practice is to wish good will for all living beings. Somewhere in the world, at any time and in many places, there are people doing this practice. You are a living being, so someone is always wishing you true happiness. In some Buddhist countries they believe that mettā is an energy, and it is directed toward those who suffer. This includes people who are not in the human realm. There are good-hearted people everywhere who want nothing more than for you to find peace and happiness.

Have a Little Conversation with Yourself

The meditation teacher Joseph Goldstein once commented on how much he likes to think, and what a problem that is for him. I don't think he is alone in that. We give our thoughts such power and importance. And when you are doing sitting meditation, it is a perfect opportunity to do just that. We aren't doing anything else, so why not think?

Some thoughts are useful. Remember the rule: anything that helps improve concentration and tranquility is helpful. You have to use the thinking process to see what is going on in your mind and to make adjustments. The Buddha called this "directed thought and evaluation." You direct your thoughts to the process of maintaining concentration, and you evaluate what is going on so you stay with the breath.

However, chances are that most of your thoughts are not of this type. And sometimes you have a problem, and you talk yourself into thinking that it is OK to work on that while you are meditating. Our mind has all sorts of rationalizations to keep us from doing what we are supposed to be doing.

Sometimes you can have a little talk with yourself. Tell yourself that yes, this is an important topic, but for this period of time it has to be put on hold. This time is precious. You can think about that problem when you are done sitting.

One of the things that can happen when the mind gets quiet is that some problems solve themselves. This is because of how the mind solves problems. People who have studied this process say that it happens in two steps. The first step is a programming phase. That is when we gather information, and this is a conscious, intellectual process. The second phase, however, happens in the subconscious. In that phase the intellectual part of the mind has to quiet down so the subconscious can do its work. This is why you can be struggling with a problem, and then you go for a walk or do housework, and minutes later the solution presents itself. You can even solve problems in your sleep.

Many people on retreat have had this happen. I have solved engineering problems that way. Figuring out how to handle family and work and life problems can happen in this way. So if you are trying to negotiate your way out of thinking about something, it might be helpful to remember that a quiet mind is pretty good at working things out.

We usually think of our minds as being one, monolithic thing. But inside our minds are many voices. It is like the cartoons where an angel is on one shoulder and the devil is on the other, and they are arguing. Unfortunately it is worse than just two voices. Ṭhānissaro Bhikkhu says that our mind is like a committee, and not a well-functioning one. It is like the "Chicago city council." That reference is little dated, but I think you get the idea. One of the things that we need to learn how to do is sort out the committee members, to make the wise ones more powerful, and stop listening to the foolish ones. We have to make the angel on our shoulder win the argument.

The Five Hindrances

The two methods I just described are not canonical. The Buddha never mentioned them. However, he did famously list the Five Hindrances to meditation:

"There are five impediments and hindrances, overgrowths of the mind that stultify insight. What five?

"Sensual desire is an impediment and hindrance, an overgrowth of the mind that stultifies insight. Ill-will... Sloth and torpor... Restlessness and remorse... Skeptical doubt are impediments and hindrances, overgrowths of the mind that stultify insight.

"Without having overcome these five, it is impossible for a monk whose insight thus lacks strength and power, to know his own true good, the good of others, and the good of both; nor

will he be capable of realizing that superhuman state of distinctive achievement, the knowledge and vision enabling the attainment of sanctity.

"But if a monk has overcome these five impediments and hindrances, these overgrowths of the mind that stultify insight, then it is possible that, with his strong insight, he can know his own true good, the good of others, and the good of both; and he will be capable of realizing that superhuman state of distinctive achievement, the knowledge and vision enabling the attainment of sanctity."
- [AN 5:51]

Sense Desire

"Suppose there were a bowl of water mixed with lac, turmeric, blue dye, or crimson dye. If a man with good sight were to examine his own facial reflection in it, he would not know and see it as it really is. So too, when one dwells with a mind obsessed and oppressed by sensual lust, and one does not understand as it really is the escape from arisen sensual lust, on that occasion one does not know and see as it really is one's own good, the good of others, and the good of both."
- [AN 5.193]

One of the fundamental teachings of the Buddha is that craving is at the root of our unhappiness. We get a thought or some sensation and suddenly we want food, sex, etc. We are overcome by a sense of wanting. We live lives that in ways subtle and not-so-subtle are dictated by our addictions. And to be clear, the Buddha's way is not about denial, but it is about freedom, being free from our habits, conditions, and cravings.

(The topic of craving is discussed in detail in *The Little Book of Buddhist Wisdom*.)

It is useful to think about craving in terms of addiction. It is something over which we do not have control. We smell food and suddenly we are hungry. We see an attractive woman or man, and we want to have sex with them. These are all compulsions. There is no free choice involved. And it gets us into all sorts of mischief. Imagine what it would be like to be free from all that.

In this case, we are talking specifically about what happens on the cushion. We have several committee members who want nothing more than to fantasize.

One thing that happens to all desires is that they fade away as our concentration improves. We replace sense desire with the pleasure born of seclusion. Seclusion has two aspects to it. The first is physical seclusion. This is why monks and nuns go off to monasteries. It is easier to quiet the mind when there are fewer distractions.

The second meaning of seclusion is seclusion from sense desire. This is an internal phenomenon. When the mind is quiet and concentrated, it is also secluded from sense desire. If the person is skilled enough, this can happen in any circumstance, even one with lots of external distractions.

The pleasure born of seclusion is free from the mischief-making that is inherent in sense desire. No one ever committed a crime or started a war because they were too serene. There are no crimes of dispassion.

Sexual desire is, of course, the most powerful type of desire. The Buddha had a few tricks to help us with those. One is to put the aging process on fast forward:

"And what, bhikkhus, is the gratification in the case of material form? Suppose there were a girl of the noble class or the brahmin class or of householder stock, in her fifteenth or sixteenth year, neither too tall nor too short, neither too thin nor too fat, neither too dark nor too fair. Is her beauty and loveliness then at its height?"

"Yes, venerable sir."

"Now the pleasure and joy that arise in dependence on that beauty and loveliness are the gratification in the case of material form.

"And what, bhikkhus, is the danger in the case of material form? Later on one might see that same woman here at eighty, ninety, or a hundred years, aged, as crooked as a roof bracket,

doubled up, supported by a walking stick, tottering, frail, her youth gone, her teeth broken, grey-haired, scanty-haired, bald, wrinkled, with limbs all blotchy. What do you think, bhikkhus? Has her former beauty and loveliness vanished and the danger become evident?"

"Yes, venerable sir."

"Bhikkhus, this is a danger in the case of material form."
- [AN 13.18-19]

This is a lesson in how fleeting and unsatisfactory physical beauty is.

Another practice for overcoming sense desire is the "contemplation of the body parts":

"...a bhikkhu reviews this same body up from the soles of the feet and down from the top of the hair, bounded by skin, as full of many kinds of impurity thus: 'In this body there are head-hairs, body-hairs, nails, teeth, skin, flesh, sinews, bones, bone-marrow, kidneys, heart, liver, diaphragm, spleen, lungs, intestines, mesentery, contents of the stomach, feces, bile, phlegm, pus, blood, sweat, fat, tears, grease, spittle, snot, oil of the joints, and urine.' Just as though there were a bag with an opening at both ends full of many sorts of grain, such as hill rice, red rice, beans, peas, millet, and white rice, and a man with good eyes were to open it and review it thus: 'This is hill rice, this is red rice, these are beans, these are peas, this is millet, this is white rice'; so too, a bhikkhu reviews this same body...as full of many kinds of impurity thus: 'In this body there are head-hairs... and urine.'"
- [MN 10.10]

Here we are invited to look into the deep nature of the body. We start with our own body. Then make this contemplation "externally," meaning that the bodies of others are exactly the same. If you strip the skin off of that attractive person, they won't look very attractive.

If these practices seem a little extreme to you, do not worry about it. Play with them if and when you feel like it. We will be going into greater detail on the teachings on impermanence and stress at a later time in *The Little Book of Buddhist Mindfulness & Concentration*.

Nonetheless, this gives you three tools to help with distraction due to sense pleasure: concentration, aging, and contemplation of body parts. Of these, concentration is certainly the most pleasant option.

Ill Will

"Suppose there were a bowl of water being heated over a fire, bubbling and boiling. If a man with good sight were to examine his own facial reflection in it, he would not know and see it as it really is. So too, when one dwells with a mind obsessed and oppressed by ill will, and one does not understand as it really is the escape from arisen ill will, on that occasion one does not know and see as it really is one's own good, the good of others, and the good of both."
- [AN 5.193]

The hindrance of ill will covers a variety of similar feelings: fear, anxiety, anger, etc. The traditional antidote to ill will is mettā, wishing good will for yourself and others.

If the problem is anxiety or fear, the method is to wish mettā for yourself, as we discussed in Establishing a Mental Posture. One thing you might try, in addition, is to place the focus on the center of the chest when you do this. That is the heart ṇ. It is the epicenter of loving-kindness. A second focal point to try is the base of the sternum, which is the center of self-confidence. This is more helpful if the problem is anxiety.

If the problem is anger or ill will toward someone else, the process is very similar. Start by feeling loving-kindness for someone you really love and care about. Get in touch with that feeling. Then transfer that feeling to the other person. Remember, everyone wants happiness. We were all babies once, and someone loved that baby, even if they are giving you problems now. This does not mean that you have to agree with them or like what they are doing. Mettā is the love that a parent has for a child. It does not necessarily mean that you approve of what they are doing. But it does mean that you will love them no matter what.

Many years ago there was a book written by Norman Mailer called *The Executioner's Song*. It is about Gary Gilmore, who was the first person put to death following a long ban on capital punishment by the Supreme Court. Gilmore was a sociopath who murdered two people.

As you can imagine, he came from a pretty dysfunctional background. But his mother, who was fully aware of what he had done and what kind of person he was, still loved him. She pleaded for mercy to the court simply on the grounds that she loved him. She asked as a mother that they not kill her only child.

This is from the "Mettā Sutta: The Discourse on Loving-kindness":

> *Even as a mother protects with her life*
> *Her child, her only child,*
> *So with a boundless heart*
> *Should one cherish all living beings;*
> - [SN 1.8]

If you find that you simply cannot feel mettā toward this person, an alternative is compassion. People who do unwholesome things suffer more from those acts than anyone else. So you can try feeling compassion for how much suffering they are causing themselves through their unskillful behavior. It is their ignorance that causes them to make their lives, now and in the future, full of great unhappiness.

If compassion does not work, try to establish equanimity. Be even-keeled. Put the problem into a bigger space. Will this be a problem in 100 years? This is not to push the problem away or act like it doesn't exist. It is just to have some perspective. Even momentous historical events fade into the past.

A week before my 18th birthday my father died. I love my father and I still think about him. But life moves on if you let it. A friend of mine uses the phrase "living around" these events. You don't act like something never happened, but you don't indulge it, either. You develop a balanced view about it.

Sloth and Torpor

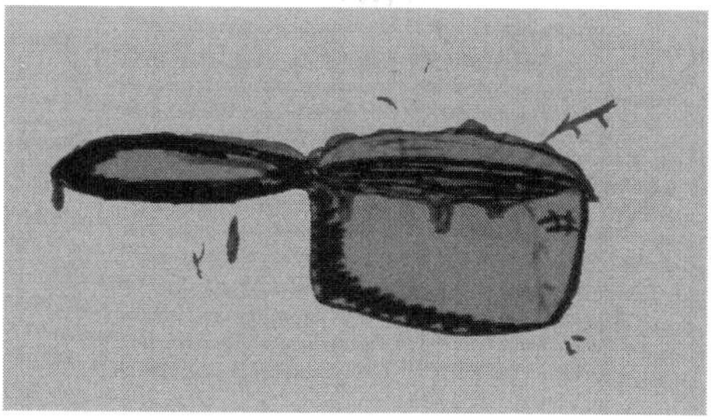

"Suppose there were a bowl of water covered over with algae and water plants. If a man with good sight were to examine his own facial reflection in it, he would not know and see it as it really is. So too, when one dwells with a mind obsessed and oppressed by dullness and drowsiness, and one does not understand as it really is the escape from arisen dullness and drowsiness, on that occasion one does not know and see as it really is one's own good, the good of others, and the good of both."
- [AN 5.193]

So you are sitting on the cushion trying your very best to keep your attention on the breath, and... zzzzzzz... you are mind-bogglingly sluggish. You may even fall asleep.

I heard a story once about a Zen master who was leading a sesshin, which is a Zen retreat. Everyone in the hall was diligently practicing, waiting for him to speak. Time went on and on and on and finally... all they could hear was the sound of him snoring.

There is a famous Buddhist from the 20th century named Dipa Ma. She was an extraordinary practitioner. She married at the age of 12. She had three children, two of whom died. Her husband, who she had come to love deeply, also died. She fell into deep despair. She was emotionally crippled. One day her doctor told her that if she did not do something to turn her life around, she would simply die.

She went to a monastery in her home country of Burma. But she was so dysfunctional that she could not even walk properly. She had to drag herself up the steps of the monastery to meditate. She later recounted that before she went to the monastery she could not sleep, and once she started to meditate, all she could do was sleep.

Sometimes the mind simply needs to shut down. It is a defense mechanism. While I am about to offer some antidotes to sloth and torpor, if you have suffered a trauma, be kind to yourself. Show yourself at least as much compassion as you would for your most beloved person.

The Buddha gave a great deal of advice on overcoming this hindrance. His most complete instructions are from the *Aṅguttara Nikāya*:

Once the Exalted One spoke to the Venerable Maha-Moggallāna thus: "Are you drowsy, Moggallāna? Are you drowsy, Moggallāna?"

"Yes, venerable sir."

"Well then, Moggallāna, at whatever thought torpor has befallen you, to that thought you should not give attention, you should not dwell on it frequently. Then it is possible that, by so doing, torpor will disappear.

"But if, by so doing, that torpor does not disappear, you should think and reflect within your mind about the Dhamma as you have heard and learned it, and you should mentally review it. Then it is possible that, by so doing, torpor will disappear.

"But if, by so doing, that torpor does not disappear, you should learn by heart the Dhamma in its fullness, as you have heard and learned it. Then it is possible...

"But if, by so doing, that torpor does not disappear, you should shake your ears, and rub your limbs with the palm of your hand. Then it is possible...

"But if, by so doing, that torpor does not disappear, you should get up from your seat, and after washing your eyes with water, you should look around in all directions and look upwards to the stars in the sky. Then it is possible...

"But if, by so doing, that torpor does not disappear, you should firmly establish the (inner) perception of light: as it is by day, so also by night; as it is by night, so also by day. Thus with a mind clear and unobstructed, you should develop a consciousness which is full of brightness. Then it is possible...

"But if, by so doing, that torpor does not disappear, you should, conscious of that which is before and behind, walk up and down, with your senses turned inwards, with your mind not going outwards. Then it is possible...

"But if, by so doing, that torpor does not disappear, you may lie down on your right side, taking up the lion's posture, covering foot with foot - mindful, clearly conscious, keeping in mind the thought of rising. Having awakened again, you should quickly rise, thinking: 'I won't indulge in the enjoyment of lying down and reclining, in the enjoyment of sleep!'

"Thus, Moggallāna, you should train yourself!"
- [AN 7:58]

Even in the fifth century BCE in India, splashing a little water on your face was a remedy for sleepiness. And notice that when all else fails, there is nothing like a little sleep.

Another antidote to sleepiness is walking meditation. We have not covered that yet, but some brisk walking can be very helpful.

Finally, although this is not canonical, a little 5 Hour Energy can help. The Buddhist monk Manoj Bhargava developed 5 Hour Energy to facilitate meditation. It was not developed as an energy drink but something for "focus," as he puts it. But the FDA would not let him market it as a "focus drink" because they do not have a category for something that helps you to concentrate.

Restlessness

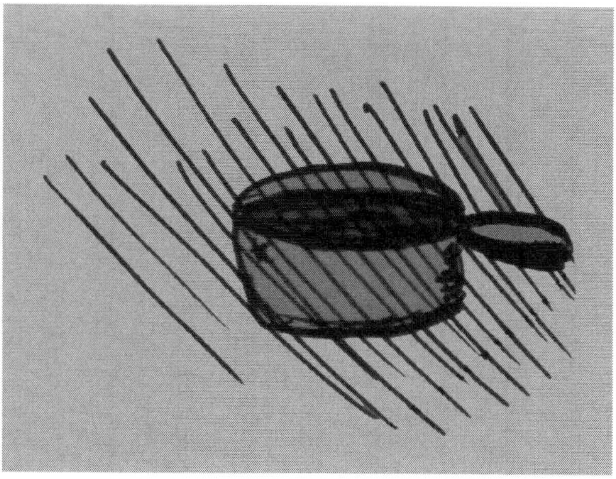

"Suppose there were a bowl of water stirred by the wind, rippling, swirling, churned into wavelets. If a man with good sight were to examine his own facial reflection in it, he would not know and see it as it really is. So too, when one dwells with a mind obsessed and oppressed by restlessness and worry, and one does not understand as it really is the escape from arisen restlessness and worry, on that occasion one does not

know and see as it really is one's own good, the good of others, and the good of both."
- [AN 5.193]

The opposite of sloth and torpor is restlessness.

There you are, sitting on your cushion, there is a statue of the Buddha on the altar, and what you see is complete serenity and that Mona Lisa half-smile on his face. This is what you want, right? You want a mind that is still and quiet and serene. And your mind and body simply won't cooperate. You are shifting and restless and your mind is going 90 mph (about 145 kph in Canada).

A number of the practices already discussed can be of help, most especially counting the breath and sweeping. Chanting, which we will discuss, can also help quiet the mind. You can do walking meditation. This can help settle the body, and that can then extend to the mind.

Restlessness will be with you for a long time. According to the Buddha, restlessness only goes away completely when you attain a full awakening. Sometimes it is helpful to just see it and not turn it into a problem.

Doubt

"Suppose there were a bowl of water that is cloudy, turbid, and muddy, placed in the dark. If a man with good sight were to examine his own facial reflection in it, he would not know and see it as it really is. So too, when one dwells with a mind obsessed and oppressed by doubt, and one does not understand as it really is the escape from arisen doubt, on that occasion one does not know and see as it really is one's own good, the good of others, and the good of both."
- [AN 5.193]

This means doubt in the Buddha's teaching and in the path that you are following. You practice and practice and practice and nothing is working. Doubt, in this case, can also mean doubt in yourself. You have faith in the path, but you are not sure that you will be able to follow it. (Hint: You can.)

Ṭhānissaro Bhikkhu says that he once went back through all of his teacher Ajahn Lee's Dharma talks and 90% of them were about encouraging his students. This is a path that is going to have its ups and downs.

The antidote to doubt is faith. A lot of Westerners do not like to hear that word, faith. But there are many kinds of faith. The kind of faith to which people usually object is blind faith, believing in something that can never be proven. In the "Cankī Sutta: With Cankī" [MN 95] the Buddha took a dim view of such faith:

"There are five things, Bhāradvāja, that may turn out in two different ways here and now. What five? Faith, approval, oral tradition, reasoned cogitation, and reflective acceptance of a view. These five things may turn out in two different ways here and now. Now something may be fully accepted out of faith, yet it may be empty, hollow, and false; but something else may not be fully accepted out of faith, yet it may be factual, true, and unmistaken. Again, something may be fully approved of... well transmitted... well cogitated... well reflected upon, yet it may be empty, hollow, and false; but something else may not be well reflected upon, yet it may be factual, true, and unmistaken. [Under these conditions] it is not proper for a wise man who preserves truth to come to the definite conclusion: 'Only this is true, anything else is wrong.'"
- [MN 95.14]

"Oral tradition" is here because in India that is how everything was transmitted. It applies equally to "written tradition," which is what we have in the West. The point the Buddha was making here is that just because something is written down does not mean that it is true.

However, we do a lot of things in life on faith. People go to college because they have faith that it will lead to a better life. Of course, there is a body of evidence that this is (sometimes? usually?) the case. But it is faith, nonetheless.

In the Buddhist tradition there is great respect for "faith followers." According to the Buddha, there are two types of people who become awakened: Dharma followers and faith followers.

The disciple enters upon the first supramundane path either as a Dhamma-follower (dhammānusārin) or as a faith-follower (saddhānusārin); the former is one in whom wisdom is the dominant faculty, the latter one who progresses by the impetus of faith.

- [Bhikkhu Ñāṇamoli; Bhikkhu Bodhi. *The Middle Length Discourses of the Buddha*, Introduction]

Faith followers have such conviction in the Dharma that they awaken simply because they believe so strongly that it will happen. Enlightenment becomes a self-fulfilling prophecy.

There is another kind of faith in Buddhism, and that is sometimes rendered as "confirmed confidence." When you start a meditation practice, you do not know if it is going to be of any value. But over time, with patience and persistence, you begin to see results. Thus, your initial faith transforms into confirmed confidence. You have some evidence that the practice is working.

One thing that can be helpful in overcoming doubt is studying the teachings of the Buddha. The Buddha's teachings hang together in a remarkably coherent way. In the *Saṃyutta Nikāya*, the Buddha described an important stage in the training where one has not yet awakened, but you have studied and pondered the Buddha's teachings enough to accept that they are true:

"Here, Mahānāma, some person does not possess confirmed confidence in the Buddha, the Dhamma, and the Saṇgha. He is not one of joyous wisdom, nor of swift wisdom, and he has not attained liberation. However, he has these five things: the faculty of faith, the faculty of energy, the faculty of mindfulness, the faculty of concentration, the faculty of wisdom. And the teachings proclaimed by the Tathāgata are accepted by him after being pondered to a sufficient degree with wisdom. This person too, Mahānāma, is one who does not go to hell, the animal realm, or the domain of ghosts, to the plane of misery, the bad destinations, the nether world."

- [SN 55.24]

For help with self-doubt, it can be helpful to read the *Theragāthā* (*Verses of the Elder Monks*) and *Therīgāthā* (*Verses of the Elder Nuns*). There are tales of the struggles that many of them had on the path. This can help you realize that you are not alone. Many of the monks and nuns had problems that are far greater than most people will ever experience. They also confirm that the result is worth it.

Another antidote that the Buddha recommends is the company of good friends. In fact, he says that this is one of the criteria for an awakening. There is this often-quoted, heart-warming passage from the *Saṃyutta Nikāya* about this subject. It starts with a statement by the Buddha's attendant Ānanda:

[Ānanda:] "Venerable sir, this is half of the holy life, that is, good friendship, good companionship, good comradeship."

[Buddha:] "Not so, Ānanda! Not so, Ānanda! This is the entire holy life, Ānanda, that is, good friendship, good companionship, good comradeship. When a bhikkhu has a good friend, a good companion, a good comrade, it is to be expected that he will develop and cultivate the Noble Eightfold Path."
- [SN 45.2]

I once had a teacher, someone with a Ph.D., who claimed that what the Buddha meant here is a metaphorical type of friendship, like a clear mind. He said that the Buddha did not mean real human beings. However, in the *Aṇguttara Nikāya* there are many passages that make it clear that what the Buddha meant by good friends is flesh and blood human beings. Here is just one of them:

"Bhikkhus, possessing eight qualities, a bhikkhu is worthy of gifts, worthy of hospitality, worthy of offerings, worthy of reverential salutation, an unsurpassed field of merit for the world. What eight?

"Here, a bhikkhu is virtuous... Having undertaken the training rules, he trains in them.

"He has learned much... and penetrated well by view.

"He has good friends, good companions, good comrades..."
- [AN 8.56]

Sometimes you can over-think things.

Summary

In this section we discussed two methods for helping to keep the mind on the breath, as well as the classic Five hindrances to meditation:

1. Breathing through the distraction.
2. Having a conversation with yourself.

The Five Hindrances:

1. Sense desire
2. Ill will
3. Sloth and torpor
4. Restlessness
5. Doubt

Mettā and the Brahma Vihāras

..."mettā" is related to the word "mitta," or friend. Universal mettā is friendliness for all. The fact that this friendliness equates with goodwill is shown in the four passages in the Canon where the Buddha recommends phrases to hold in mind to develop thoughts of mettā. These phrases provide his clearest guide not only to the heart-quality that underlies mettā, but also to the understanding of happiness that explains why it's wise and realistic to develop mettā for all.

- [Ṭhānissaro Bhikkhu, "When Goodwill is Better than Love: The Meaning of 'Metta'", Shambhala Sun, July 10, 2011]

The cultivation of mettā is part of a larger practice, that of the "brahma vihāras." The word "brahma" means "noble," and the word "vihāra" means "dwelling place." Thus, "brahma vihāra" is usually translated as something like "noble abiding."

The brahma vihāras are loving-kindness (mettā), compassion (karuṇā), sympathetic joy (muditā), and equanimity (uppekhā). The Buddha described them in this way:

"Then, with his heart filled with loving-kindness, he dwells suffusing one quarter, the second, the third, the fourth. Thus he dwells suffusing the whole world, upwards, downwards, across, everywhere, always with a heart filled with loving-kindness, abundant, unbounded, without hate or ill-will.

"Just as if a mighty trumpeter were with little difficulty to make a proclamation to the four quarters, so by this meditation, Vasettha, by this liberation of the heart through loving-kindness he leaves nothing untouched, nothing unaffected in the sensuous sphere. This, Vasettha, is the way to union with Brahmā.

"Then with his heart filled with compassion... with sympathetic joy, with equanimity he dwells suffusing one quarter, the second, the third, the fourth. Thus he dwells suffusing the whole world, upwards, downwards, across, everywhere, always with a heart filled with equanimity, abundant, unbounded, without hate or ill-will."

- [DN 13.76-78]

Here the Buddha described all four of the brahma vihāras. However, as a formal practice, mettā is the quality that gets the most emphasis. The "Mettā Sutta" [SN 1.8] is chanted regularly around the world.

Mettā

The Pāli commentaries say that the Buddha originally gave the instructions on mettā to monks who were harassed by the tree spirits of a forest in which the monks were trying to meditate. After doing this meditation, the spirits were so affected by the power of benevolence that they allowed the monks to stay in the forest for the duration of the rainy season retreat. (Internet search: "metta buddharakkhita")

As is often the case with anything that comes out of India, the distinction between myth and reality is blurred. However, I think the point is clear. Meeting conflict with conflict has an obvious result. Meeting conflict with love, compassion, and wisdom may have a somewhat better result. Of course, we are not wired in this way, and it takes a leap of faith, as well as some courage and conviction, to meet conflict with love, compassion, and equanimity.

The Buddha himself did not give a formal practice on how to cultivate mettā or any of the brahma vihāras. However, over time various practices evolved. For a classic treatment of mettā practice in the Burmese tradition, you may want to read Sharon Salzberg's book *Loving-kindness, the Revolutionary Art of Happiness*. Here I will give the instructions in brief.

The main practice consists of two parts: mettā phrases that are repeated and a mettā recipient.

Because the phrases are not canonical, you can really use anything that you like. The purpose is to establish a quality of heart, a feeling of unbounded love.

The important thing, therefore, is not that you repeat these phrases over and over in some mechanical way. That would hardly be useful. The most important thing is that quality of heart, the feeling of love. This is why I recommend that you begin by thinking of someone you love unconditionally, someone for whom you wish only unbounded happiness. Children and babies work well. Animals work well. Anyone for whom you have deep feelings of love and gratitude works well. As you think of them, get in touch with that feeling, especially at the heart center, the heart ṇ, located at the center of the chest. Use the heart center as the focal point for the breath.

Once you have established the feeling of unbounded love, start by directing that feeling toward yourself, repeating the phrases:

> *May I be free from danger.*
> *May I be happy.*
> *May I be healthy.*
> *May I be at ease.*

Repeat them for a few minutes, as long as you like. As usual, this is not a race. Settle into the phrases and the feeling of loving-kindness.

Next, you direct mettā to a benefactor, someone who has been a loving and kind supporter to you:

> *May [they] be free from danger.*
> *May [they] be happy.*
> *May [they] be healthy.*
> *May [they] be at ease.*

Next comes a beloved friend:

> *May [they] be free from danger.*
> *May [they] be happy.*
> *May [they] be healthy.*
> *May [they] be at ease.*

The first three recipients of mettā are easy. These are people we love and care about.

Next comes a neutral person. This can be difficult. There are very few people about whom we have neither positive nor negative feelings. It may be someone who works in a shop or a neighbor who you do not know well. It may take a little time to come up with a person for whom you have neutral feelings:

> *May [they] be free from danger.*
> *May [they] be happy.*
> *May [they] be healthy.*
> *May [they] be at ease.*

The next one is the hardest one. In the commentaries, this person is rather dramatically called the "enemy." It is probably not too hard to come up with this person:

May [they] be free from danger.
May [they] be happy.
May [they] be healthy.
May [they] be at ease.

And finally, we direct mettā toward all beings, seen and unseen:

May all beings be free from danger.
May all beings be happy.
May all beings be healthy.
May all beings be at ease.

Clearly, wishing good will toward an enemy is the most difficult one. You may want to review the section on Ill Will in the chapter on Problems While Meditating.

The most important thing about mettā is that you understand that this is a quality to develop. For negative mind states like anxiety, anger, ill will, fear, etc., the antidote is mettā.

Here is also a good opportunity to say something about our minds and the issue of how they develop over a lifetime. In Buddhism we often use the word "practice." This is to indicate that we are working at something and to get better at it.

But we are always practicing something. Every time that something manifests in the mind, our predisposition for that mind state gets stronger. If we have a lot of anger, every time that we get angry, that strengthens the potential for anger. The next time the proper causes and conditions are in place, the anger will manifest even more quickly. This is why someone who is 20 years old who has a lot of anger will get angrier and angrier. By the time they are 60 or 80 no one can stand to be around them anymore. They have had a lot of time to practice, and they get really good at it.

What I just described is a mindless kind of practice. There is no self-awareness. What we are trying to cultivate is a mindful practice, one where we are clear about the qualities we want to develop in the mind. Simply knowing that we want to cultivate the brahma vihāras is important.

Compassion

As mentioned before, and not surprisingly, directing mettā toward an enemy can be very challenging. In this case, directing compassion toward that person may work better. Thich Nhat Hanh defines love as the "intention and the capacity to make people happy." He defines compassion (karuṇā) as the "intention and the capacity to ease peoples' suffering." And when people are difficult, no one suffers because of that more than they do.

One example of this is driving. Everyone has experienced being cut off by an aggressive driver. But long after you have forgotten about it, that person still has to live inside that angry, unhappy mind. So you can feel happy that you are not like that, and you can feel compassion for someone who has to suffer from that mind.

Sympathetic Joy

The next brahma vihāra is muditā (Pāli). This is usually translated as "sympathetic joy." In English, we don't even have a word for it. We do have a word for its opposite, and that is jealousy. We even have a more dramatic version which is "schadenfreude." That is delighting in someone's misfortune. Muditā is feeling the same amount of joy for someone else's happiness as we do for our own. So if someone has wonderful good fortune, we feel as happy for them as we would if that good fortune had come our way. It is a feeling that can only come from selflessness.

Equanimity

Finally, there is equanimity. This is the feeling of being even-keeled. We are neither repulsed by the negative nor attracted by the positive.

Many people confuse equanimity with indifference. In Buddhist psychology there is the notion of near and far enemies. Far enemies are qualities that are the opposite of something. So the far enemy of "love" is "hate." The far enemy of "compassion" is "cruelty." Those are rather obvious. The near enemy of "love" is "attachment." Attachment masquerades as love but is really self-serving. It is about what we want, not what someone else needs. The near enemy of "compassion" is "pity."

And the near enemy of "equanimity" is "indifference." Equanimity is not indifferent. It is more like "if you can keep your head when all about you are losing theirs" [Kipplinq].

Thich Nhat Hanh tells this story. In an incident that has been somewhat lost to history, in 1976 and 1977 many refugees fled the tyranny of the political regime in Cambodia. They left in overloaded, flimsy, rotting boats, many of which sank, and many thousands of people died.

However, some boats survived, and afterward someone studied why certain boats made it and some did not. There was one common denominator, and that was if there was just one person on a boat who did not panic, that boat had a very high chance of success.

This is equanimity in the purest sense, supported by courage, love, and compassion.

Summary

One of the traditional mettā practices is described here. However, the most important point about the brahma vihāras is to recognize them as qualities to develop. And you will find that as your concentration and tranquility develop, the brahma vihāras will begin to manifest on their own. A mind that is at peace with itself will naturally incline toward altruism. The calm, happy, tranquil mind has no need for greed, hatred, and jealousy.

Additional Aids in Meditation

Walking Meditation

...it was the Buddha himself who first taught walking meditation. In the Great Discourse on the Foundations of Mindfulness, the Buddha taught walking meditation two times. In the section called "Postures," he said that a monk knows "I am walking" when he is walking, knows "I am standing" when he is standing, knows "I am sitting" when he is sitting, and knows "I am lying down" when he is lying down. In another section called "Clear Comprehension," the Buddha said, "A monk applies clear comprehension in going forward and in going back." Clear comprehension means the correct understanding of what one observes. To correctly understand what is observed, a yogi must gain concentration, and in order to gain concentration, he must apply mindfulness. Therefore, when the Buddha said, "Monks, apply clear comprehension," we must understand that not only clear comprehension must be applied, but also mindfulness and concentration. Thus the Buddha was instructing meditators to apply mindfulness, concentration, and clear comprehension while walking, while "going forward and back." Walking meditation is thus an important part of this process.

- [Sayadaw U Silananda, "The Benefits of Walking Meditation"]

I have gotten a lot of instruction over the years on walking meditation. However, the best instruction I got was not at a meditation retreat; it was in a Tai Chi class.

Walking meditation has some of the same aims as sitting meditation, mainly a) keeping your attention in the present moment and b) maintaining a broad-based sense of awareness. As you might suspect, it is a body practice.

Sometimes the walking meditation instructions are to keep your attention very narrowly focused, like in the soles of the feet. But this is not what we are looking for, and it is certainly very hard to go through the day in normal activities trying to keep a narrow focus like that. You'll start walking into walls. One of the purposes of walking meditation is to bring the practice into daily life. So try to keep the same kind of broad-based attention that you are working on in the sitting meditation. The main difference is that the 80-20 rule will be 80% of your attention on walking and 20% on the breath. Your main focus of attention is the whole body.

The typical way to do walking meditation is to start by finding a place where you can take 20-30 steps. Walk from one end of that space to the other, then turn around and go back the other way. Your objective is to take those 20-30 steps without losing your attention on the walking and the breath.

In Tai Chi walking, when you take a step, you transfer all of your weight onto the foot, and then put your weight on that foot in such a way that the other leg can swing freely. You balance completely on one leg. You may even want to swing that leg back and forth a few times to make sure that you are properly balanced. Then you take the free leg and step out, still keeping all of your weight on the other leg. Likewise, to make sure that this is the case, you can bring the free leg back and forth a few times. Then you step forward and transfer all of your weight onto the other leg, making sure that you keep everything completely balanced. One way to think of it is to imagine that you are walking on a high wire.

Transferring your weight completely from one leg to the other helps keep your attention completely focused on the walking. That is why I prefer Tai Chi walking as walking meditation.

Try to get your walking in sync with your breathing. You can play with this. Take one breath for each step or two breaths for each step. Or take two steps for each breath. There are no rules other than maintaining your attention. If you are feeling tired, you may want to walk as quickly as possible to generate some energy. If you are restless, you may also want to walk quickly to burn off some energy. Some people think that very slow walking is more "spiritual." There are no bonus points for slow walking. Adjust your walking speed to match the needs of the mind and body.

There are several types of Tai Chi walking. You should feel free to explore them. There are some very good instructions on the Internet (Internet search: "tai chi walking marantz"). But as a meditation exercise, the aim is to keep transferring your weight from one leg to the other and maintain your weight and balance on one leg at a time.

If you want to raise the stakes, a very interesting advanced exercise is to use the old "balance a book on your head" routine. This requires even more concentration. But it also can make it more fun, even a little silly.

Finally, you may find that this type of walking makes the muscles stiffen. This is another case where doing some stretching afterward is beneficial.

Guided Meditations

There are many guided meditations available on the Internet. Guided meditations are particularly helpful if you are having a hard time maintaining focus.

Ṭhānissaro Bhikkhu has a plethora of short Dharma talks that he gives at the beginning of their evening, one-hour meditation sessions. They usually run from 10-15 minutes. I highly recommended them. You can find them at *dhammatalks.org* in the section labeled "talks→evening talks."

One of the really wonderful Dharma teachers of the 20th century was Ayya Khema. She has many talks and guided meditations at the website *dharmaseed.org*. There are two sets of guided meditations on mettā called "Loving Kindness Classic" (Internet search: "ayya khema loving kindness classic") and "Loving Kindness New Style" (Internet search: "ayya khema loving kindness new style"). I highly recommend all of her teachings.

There are many other guided meditations on the Internet, but be aware of whether they are consistent with these particular instructions. You may find yourself running into conflicts if they are not.

There are a number of chakra guided meditations (Internet search: "chakra cleansing activating guided meditation") on YouTube. Just keep in mind that strictly speaking, chakra practice is Hindu, and Hinduism has some different beliefs from Buddhism (most notably "self" vs. "non-self"). Nonetheless, if you can tune out the theism and the self-ness, these can be helpful.

Finally, there are also guided concentration meditations (Internet search: "concentration complete exercise"), some of which use breath counting. Look for these as another supplement to what is here.

Gāthās

A "gāthā" is a poem. We have already seen this word in the book names *Theragāthā* and *Therīgāthā*.

Gāthās have been used for many years to keep the mind focused. In some Zen traditions, there are gāthās for everything from getting up in the morning to brushing your teeth to eating to doing the dishes. There is a gāthā for almost everything (Internet search: "thich nhat hanh gathas here and now").

As with the mettā phrases, you repeat them silently to yourself. Thich Nhat Hanh teaches this one for mindfulness meditation:

> *Breathing in, I know I am breathing in.*
> *Breathing out, I know I am breathing out.*
> *As my in-breath grows deep,*
> *my out-breath grows slow.*
> *Breathing in, I calm my body.*
> *Breathing out, I feel ease.*
> *Breathing in, I smile.*
> *Breathing out, I release.*
> *Dwelling in the present moment,*
> *I know this is a wonderful moment.*

You say the odd-numbered phrases on the in-breath and the even-numbered phrases on the out-breath.

(Ṭhānissaro Bhikkhu notes that not every moment is wonderful. But I think the idea here is clear, and that is to use this as a way to help calm the mind.)

There are gāthās for getting out of bed, washing your hands, washing the dishes, and so on. Thich Nhat Hanh also teaches that when you do the dishes, do them as if you are washing the baby Buddha. It is a lovely thought.

It is not so much that you need to memorize every gāthā. The idea is to bring your undivided attention to every moment of the day. You use the breath to help in this way. And I think you will find that every time you find the breath, that it will have a calming effect on the mind. The day simply becomes less stressful.

* * *

Meditation in Daily Life

Apropos of the discussion on gāthās, this practice does not have much meaning if it is limited to the cushion. You should bring the practice into everything you do. You can use the 80-20 rule to bring the breath into almost any activity. Remember, the objective is not to put your attention fully on the breath. The objective is to use the breath to keep you fully in the present moment. In this way you can bring more awareness to your thoughts, speech, and actions.

Summary

In this section, we added a number of techniques to our meditation toolbox. These include:

1. Walking meditation
2. Guided meditations
3. Gāthās
4. Using the breath during the day to bring mindfulness into every moment

Chanting

There is a saying in Tibet that a beautiful voice can make a wild animal stop dead in its tracks and listen.

- [Mary Talbot, "Yungchen Llamo: Melodies from the Meditative State", Tricycle Magazine, Spring 1997]

Chanting has been a part of Buddhist practice since the time of the Buddha. Because it was an oral tradition, the monks and nuns memorized the Buddha's discourses. The discourses were often composed in verse form. This lent them particularly well to chanting. The traditional language for chanting in the southern tradition of Buddhism is Pāli. Pāli has a unique rhythmic quality to it, something akin to Italian in the West.

Chanting is not as common in Western Buddhism as it is in the East. Some of that is cultural. Westerners do not seem comfortable with chanting. I went to a retreat with Thich Nhat Hanh once where after a few days some people started grousing about how they were being "forced to chant." His response was, "To chant or not to chant; that is not a question."

If chanting really makes you uncomfortable, then don't do it. But remember that we are doing this practice as a way of pushing up against our boundaries. Chanting won't hurt you, really, and it may help. So when you feel ready to revisit this practice, please do.

There are some good reasons to include chanting in your daily practice. The first of these is that chanting can help to quiet the mind and bring you into the present moment. When you first sit down, you may have many things on your mind. Getting the mind to settle down is probably difficult. Chanting can help you let go of those worldly distractions, remind you what you are doing and why, and bring your mind fully into the meditation.

Another important reason is that chanting embeds the teachings in your mind. If you memorize a chant, then when you are out during the day, there will be moments when the words of the chant will come to mind. The chant may help you to act in a more skillful way. This is why the monks and nuns chant the *Pātimokkha* (the monastic code) on the full moon and new moon days. Chanting helps commit the teachings to memory and to put them front and center into our consciousness.

Finally, chanting connects us to a long and honored tradition. Since the day the Buddha first taught the Four Noble Truths, Buddhists have chanted the discourses. When I was in India, I heard hundreds of Sri Lankan pilgrims chant the "Dhammacakkappavattana Sutta: The Four Noble Truths" [SN 56.11] at the Mulagandhakuti Vihāra in Sarnath. They had it memorized. It was a transcendent experience. In moments like that we were all connected as part of this great tradition.

There are many chants. You should choose ones that you like. There is no right or wrong list of chants to do. The ones that I picked out here are ones that I enjoy, and they facilitate the practice. These chants are well-known in the Buddhist world, and they are part of the standard repertoire.

The easiest way to chant is to have a recording of the chant and its text. You can just chant in English if you like, but I enjoy the rhythm of the Pāli language. I also think it helps to connect you more deeply to the Buddhist tradition. As you will see in the recommended list of chants, some are in Pāli only, some are in Pāli and English, and some are just in English. If you are doing the Pāli only chants, make sure that you know the meaning of the words. Otherwise the chant will not be very helpful in your practice.

Pāli Pronunciation

Pāli is unique in that it is a spoken language with no native alphabet. You may know that Chinese is just the opposite; it is a language where there is a standard written form, but the words have different spoken forms. As Buddhism moved from country to country, it used whatever the native alphabet was.

When Western scholars started studying Pāli, they had to solve the problem of a written alphabet. The solution is "Romanized Pāli." The Pāli language has 41 characters in it. Because the Roman alphabet only has 26 letters, the other characters are represented using diacritical marks.

There are a number of differences between Indic languages and English. The first is that Indic languages are built more scientifically. They arrange letters in the alphabet by where in the mouth the sound occurs. For example, ḍ, ḷ, ṇ, and ṭ are "palatal consonants." They are pronounced with the tongue touching the roof of the mouth. The characters d, l, n, and t are lengua-dental consonants. They are pronounced with the tongue touching the teeth.

(The letter ḍ is called "d dot under.")

Second, Indic languages do not have a "th" sound as in the word "this." What they do have is a sound with a character followed by an "h". In that sound, there is a slight puff of air that follows the consonant. These are "aspirated consonants." The letter "th" is a "t" sound followed by a puff of air.

Finally, in Indic languages, the default accent is on the third to last syllable. In the Pāli word "nimitta" ("sign"), the accent is on "ni." However, in most Pāli words the default accent is over-ridden by the rules for vowel pronunciation. In the word "bhāvanā" ("meditation") both "a's" are long and have equal emphasis.

Here is how to pronounce the vowels:

"a" as in "but"

"i" as in "pin"

"u" as in "duke"

"ā" as in "father"

"ī" as in "keen"

"ū" as in "pool"

"e" as in "way"

"o" as in "home"

Here is how to pronounce the consonants:

"g" is pronounced as in "girl"

"c" as in "church"

"ñ" as in "canyon"

Here is how to pronounce the "cerebrals":

"ṭ, ḍ, ṇ" are spoken with the tongue on the roof of the mouth. These are called "dentals"

"t, d, n, l" with the tongue on the upper teeth

"ṃ" is a nasal as in "sing"

Here is how to pronounce the "aspirates":

"kh, gh, ch, jh, ṭh, ḍh, th, dh, ph bh" pronounced with a slight outward puff of breath, e.g., "th" as in "Thomas" (not as in "that"), "ph" as in "top hat" (not as in "phone")

Double consonants are always enunciated separately, e.g., "dd" as in "mad dog," "gg" as in "big gun"

An "o" and an "e" always carry a stress, otherwise the stress falls on a long vowel: "ā, ī, ū", or on a double consonant, or on "ṃ".

(Most of this information comes from the Introduction to the *Majjhima Nikāya* by Bhikkhu Bodhi.)

Homage to the Buddha

Traditionally, the first chant is "Homage to the Buddha." This is repeated three times. Doing something three times in India and in Buddhist practice gives it a seal of authority. These first three chants are typically done in Pāli only. The translations are underneath the Pāli. They are typically done together, although the first chant is often done separately at the beginning of any Dharma related activity like a Dharma talk.

Namo tassa bhagavato arahato sammā-sambuddhassa
(Homage to the blessed, noble and perfectly enlightened one.)

Namo tassa bhagavato arahato sammā-sambuddhassa
(Homage to the blessed, noble and perfectly enlightened one.)

Namo tassa bhagavato arahato sammā-sambuddhassa
(Homage to the blessed, noble and perfectly enlightened one.)

Going for Refuge

In the next one you go for refuge, a safe haven, in the Three Jewels: the Buddha, the Dharma, and the Saṅgha. These are also done three times. This chant is also usually done in Pāli only.

Buddhaṃ saraṇaṃ gacchāmi
(To the Buddha, I go for refuge.)

Dhammaṃ saraṇaṃ gacchāmi
(To the Dhamma, I go for refuge.)

Saṇghaṃ saraṇaṃ gacchāmi
(To the Saṇgha, I go for refuge.)

Dutiyampi Buddhaṃ saraṇaṃ gacchāmi
(For the second time I take refuge in the Buddha.)

Dutiyampi Dhammaṃ saraṇaṃ gacchāmi
(For the second time I take refuge in the Dhamma.)

Dutiyampi Saṇghaṃ saraṇaṃ gacchāmi
(For the second time I take refuge in the Saṇgha.)

Tatiyampi Buddhaṃ saraṇaṃ gacchāmi
(For the third time I take refuge in the Buddha.)

Tatiyampi Dhammaṃ saraṇaṃ gacchāmi
(For the third time I take refuge in the Dhamma.)

Tatiyampi Saṇghaṃ saraṇaṃ gacchāmi
(For the third time I take refuge in the Saṇgha.)

The Five Precepts

Then you take the five ethical and moral precepts. These are discussed in *The Little Book of Buddhist Virtue*. For now, you can see what they look like, even if you prefer not to chant them until you understand them. This chant is here in Pāli only, but it is also commonly done in both Pāli and English.

Pāṇatipātā veramaṇī sikkhāpadaṃ samādiyāmi.
(I undertake the precept to refrain from taking the life of any living creature.)

Adinnādānā veramaṇī sikkhāpadaṃ samādiyāmi.
(I undertake the precept to refrain from taking that which is not given.)

Kāmesu micchācārā veramaṇī sikkhāpadaṃ samādiyāmi.
(I undertake the precept to refrain from sexual misconduct.)

Musāvādā veramaṇī sikkhāpadaṃ samādiyāmi.
(I undertake the precept to refrain from false and harmful speech.)

Surāmeraya-majja-pamādatthānā veramaṇī sikkhāpadaṃ samādiyāmi.

(I undertake the precept to refrain from consuming intoxicating drink and drugs, which lead to heedlessness.)

There is a lovely recording of these three chants by Upāsikā Sobhanā at the Birken Forest Monastery in British Columbia, Canada. (Internet search: "youtube homage refuge precepts")

Five Subjects for Frequent Recollection

The next three chants are from the chant book of Abhayagiri Monastery (Internet search: "abhayagiri chant book"). The chant book also has up and down arrows that show whether the tone is high or low. Chanting is typically done with three tones: a mid-tone, a high tone, and a low one.

In the chapter on Establishing a Mental Posture, one of the steps is the "Five Subjects for Frequent Recollection." This is the "Upajjhatthana Sutta: Contemplations" [AN 5.57]. Here are two versions of the chant. One is for women and has the feminine word forms, and the second version has the masculine word forms. The words that are gender-specific are in bold.

This chant is in both Pāli and English. The lines in square brackets ([...]) are usually only chanted by the chant leader.

Chant for women:

[Handa mayaṃ abhiṇha-paccavekkhaṇa-pāṭaṃ bhaṇāmase]
[Jarā-dhammomhi] jaraṃ ***anatītā***
I am of the nature to age, I have not gone beyond aging.

Byādhī-dhammomhi byādhiṃ ***anatītā***
I am of the nature to sicken, I have not gone beyond sickness.

ṃṇa-dhammomhi maraṇaṃ ***anatītā***
I am of the nature to die, I have not gone beyond dying.

Sabbehi me piyehi manāpehi nānābhāvo vinābhāvo
All that is mine, beloved and pleasing, will become otherwise, will become separated from me.

Kammassakāmhi kammadāyādā *kammayoni kammabandhu kamma-**paṭisaranā**.*
Yaṃ kammaṃ karissāmi kalyāṇaṃ vā pāpakaṃ vā tassa ***dāyādā****bhavissāmi*

I am the owner of my kamma, heir to my kamma, born of my kamma, related to my kamma, abide supported by my kamma. Whatever kamma I shall do, for good or for ill, of that I will be the heir.

Evaṃ amhehi abhiṇhaṃ paccavekkhitabbaṃ
Thus we should frequently recollect.

Chant for men:

[Handa mayaṃ abhiṇha-paccavekkhaṇa-pāṭaṃ bhaṇāmase]
[Jarā-dhammomhi] jaraṃ ***anatīto***
I am of the nature to age, I have not gone beyond aging.

Byādhī-dhammomhi byādhiṃ ***anatīto***
I am of the nature to sicken, I have not gone beyond sickness.

Maraṇa-dhammomhi maraṇaṃ ***anatīto***
I am of the nature to die, I have not gone beyond dying.

Sabbehi me piyehi manāpehi nānābhāvo vinābhāvo
All that is mine, beloved and pleasing, will become otherwise, will become separated from me.

Kammassakomhi kammādāyādo *kammayoni kammabandhu kamma-****paṭisarano****.*
Yaṃ kammaṃ karissāmi kalyāṇaṃ vā pāpakaṃ vā tassa ***dāyādo****bhavissāmi*
I am the owner of my kamma, heir to my kamma, born of my kamma, related to my kamma, abide supported by my kamma. Whatever kamma I shall do, for good or for ill, of that I will be the heir.

Evaṃ amhehi abhiṇhaṃ paccavekkhitabbaṃ
Thus we should frequently recollect.

You can find audio for this chant by doing an Internet search on "abhayagiri five subjects chant." Because monks are chanting, the audio has the masculine forms.

The Mettā Sutta

The next one is the "Karaṇīya Mettā Sutta: The Buddha's Words on Loving-kindness" [AN 11.15]. This one is very commonly done, even in groups that do not normally do chanting. It helps to firmly establish the quality of loving-kindness in the mind. This one is in English only.

[This is what should be done]
By one who is skilled in goodness
And who knows the path of peace:
Let them be able and upright,
Straightforward and gentle in speech,
Humble and not conceited,
Contented and easily satisfied,
Unburdened with duties and frugal in their ways.
Peaceful and calm, and wise and skillful,
Not proud and demanding in nature.
Let them not do the slightest thing
That the wise would later reprove,
Wishing, in gladness and in safety,
May all beings be at ease.
Whatever living beings there may be,
Whether they are weak or strong, omitting none,
The great or the mighty, medium, short, or small,
The seen and the unseen,
Those living near and far away,
Those born and to be born,
May all beings be at ease.
Let none deceive another
Or despise any being in any state.
Let none through anger or ill-will
Wish harm upon another.
Even as a mother protects with her life
Her child, her only child,
So with a boundless heart
Should one cherish all living beings,
Radiating kindness over the entire world:
Spreading upwards to the skies
And downwards to the depths,
Outwards and unbounded,
Freed from hatred and ill-will.
Whether standing or walking, seated or lying down,
Free from drowsiness,
One should sustain this recollection.
This is said to be the sublime abiding.
By not holding to fixed views,
The pure-hearted one, having clarity of vision,
Being freed from all sense-desires,
Is not born again into this world.

You can find audio for this chant by doing an Internet search on "abhayagiri metta chant."

The Highest Blessings

The last chant is the "Maṇgala Sutta: Highest Blessings" [Khp 5]. In this sutta, notice how the Buddha starts with the blessings of worldly life and works his way up to final liberation, nirvāṇa.

[Thus have I heard that the Blessed One]
Was staying at Sāvātthī,
Residing at the Jeta's Grove
In Anāthapiṇḍika's park.
Then in the dark of the night, a radiant deva
Illuminated all Jeta's Grove.
She bowed down low before the Blessed One
Then standing to one side she said:
Devas are concerned for happiness
And ever long for peace.
The same is true for humankind.
What then are the highest blessings?
Avoiding those of foolish ways,
Associating with the wise,
And honoring those worthy of honor.
These are the highest blessings.
Living in places of suitable kinds,
With the fruits of past good deeds
And guided by the rightful way.
These are the highest blessings.
Accomplished in learning and craftsman's skills,
With discipline, highly trained,
And speech that is true and pleasant to hear.
These are the highest blessings.
Providing for mother and father's support
And cherishing family,
And ways of work that harm no being,
These are the highest blessings.
Giving with Dhamma in the heart,
Offering help to relatives and kin,
And acting in ways that leave no blame.
These are the highest blessings.
Steadfast in restraint, and shunning evil ways,

Avoiding intoxicants that dull the mind,
And heedfulness in all things that arise.
These are the highest blessings.
Respectfulness and of humble ways,
Contentment and gratitude,
And hearing the Dhamma frequently taught.
These are the highest blessings.
Patience and willingness to accept one's faults,
Seeing venerated seekers of the truth,
And sharing often the words of Dhamma.
These are the highest blessings.
The Holy Life lived with ardent effort,
Seeing for oneself the Noble Truths,
And the realization of Nibbāna.
These are the highest blessings.
Although involved in worldly ways,
Unshaken the mind remains
And beyond all sorrow, spotless, secure.
These are the highest blessings.
They who live by following this path
Know victory wherever they go,
And every place for them is safe.
These are the highest blessings.

You can find audio for this chant by doing an Internet search on "abhayagiri highest blessings chant."

Summary

In this chapter, we discussed the reasons why chanting is beneficial to your practice:

1. Chanting helps to settle the mind.
2. Chanting helps embed the teachings into your mind.
3. Chanting helps you connect to the tradition and to practicing Buddhists around the world.

Next, we introduced six chants that are part of the standard repertoire. These are:

1. Homage to the Buddha.
2. Going for refuge.

3. The five precepts.
4. Five subjects for frequent recollection.
5. The discourse on loving-kindness.
6. The discourse on the highest blessings.

All six of these chants concatenated together are available on the Internet. (Search keywords: "daily pali meditation chants")

Postscript

This ends the description of how to establish a daily meditation practice. While the book is short, there are many practices here, and it will take a while for you to become familiar with all of them. The goal at this stage of your practice is to establish a sense of well-being. Try to enjoy your meditation and not to be overly serious about it.

You may be the type of person who is naturally happy, calm, and contented. That would make you a very rare individual. But many of us, and I am guessing most of us, come into the world wounded. And even if we do not start out that way, we usually accumulate some wounds in the course of our lives.

So in the beginning, the objective of meditation is to heal. We want to create an emotional home base for ourselves, a place of quiet, serenity, and security.

This will, of course, take time. The mind will want to do two things. First, it will want to run around like crazy. It will resist staying on the breath. It feels threatened there. And every time a thought or a sound or a feeling arises, the mind will chase after it. This is what the mind normally does, and slowly and persistently and compassionately we want to bring the attention back to the breath.

The second thing the mind will do is to obsess on our wounds. That person who is giving us trouble in life or that unhappy situation will show up again and again and again. Our minds will grab onto a difficult experience, and it will spin and spin and spin. And each time it spins, the centrifugal force of the spinning will make it go faster.

The solution in both cases is to come gently, quietly, and compassionately back to the breath.

Eventually, you will have a moment of stillness. It will probably be very fleeting. But when that happens, see it. This is where you want to go.

To be sure, this is not all there is to meditation. There are many, many practices designed to help us out of our problems in life. But this is where we begin. You build a house by starting with the foundation. If the foundation is strong, the house has a good start on being strong itself. But a weak foundation will almost surely cause the house to fall down, no matter how well the rest of the house is built.

We need a home base. The way we do this is simplicity itself. We start by following the breath at the nose. We feel the air coming in and going out.

Next we expand our sense of awareness to include the whole body. The whole body breathes in, and the whole body breathes out. We keep our primary attention on the nose, and we keep our secondary attention on the whole body. Over time, the sense of the physical body becomes less pronounced than the feeling of the breath-body, the energy field that encompasses the body. The breath is no longer the air coming and the air going out. It is an energy field that pulses with each in-breath and each out-breath.

And finally we expand even that sense of awareness to the mind. We use the attention on the breath-body to quiet the mind, to still the thoughts until they become just a whisper.

These moments will come and they will go, but this is what we are after. And it is in this field of calm and stillness and silence that we begin to heal. This is how we establish the foundation in which the following stages in our meditation can grow. And when we inevitably backslide in those stages, we have a place to return that is safe and secure.

The Buddha used the simile of a bathman who takes soap powder and soaks it with water until every grain of powder is suffused with water:

"Just as a skilled bathman or his assistant, kneading the soap-powder which he has sprinkled with water, forms from it, in a metal dish, a soft lump, so that the ball of soap-powder becomes one oleaginous mass, bound with oil so that nothing escapes — so this monk suffuses, drenches, fills and irradiates his body so that no spot remains untouched. This, Sire, is a fruit of the homeless life, visible here and now, that is more excellent and perfect than the former ones."
- [DN 2.76]

When this first happens to you, it may only happen for the space of one breath, or even half a breath. Your mind will pull back, and that is fine. The habitual mind doesn't want to go there. But as always, come back to the breath calmly, quietly, and with compassion. Your mind has a very bad habit, and that is to perpetuate its own suffering. In order to help your mind out of its dilemma, you must hold it gently like a baby or a kitten, and you must hold it with love. And then you must usher it back to the breath, gently and firmly, to a place of healing.

So this, then, is the beginning of a lifelong meditation practice. It is a place of love, a place of friendship, and a place of security. It does not harm anyone or anything, and because it is completely yours, you can take it with you wherever you go.

Those who
Fully cultivate the Factors of Awakening,
Give up grasping,
Enjoy non-clinging,
And have destroyed the toxins,
Are luminous,
And completely liberated in this life.
- [Dhp 89]

Appendices

Appendix A - Glossary of Terms

Abhidhamma (Pāli, Sanskrit: Abhidharma)
The *Abhidhamma* is the third of the "three baskets" in the Pāli Canon, although scholars date it to 100 to 200 years after the time of the Buddha. It has been variously described as philosophy, psychology, and metaphysics. The *Abhidhamma* is highly revered in the Theravada tradition, and highly criticized in the others (!).

Ajahn (also Ajaan)
Thai word meaning "teacher." In Buddhism it is a monk who has at least ten years of seniority.

Aṇguttara Nikāya
Literally "Increased by One Collection," but usually translated as "Numerical Discourses." It is the second of the five *nikāyas*, or collections, in the Sutta Pitaka of the Pāli Canon. The Aṇguttara Nikāya is organized in eleven books according to the number of items referenced in them (i.e., the Four Noble Truths is in the Book of Fours).

arahant (Pāli, Sanskrit: arahat)
Literally "one who is worthy," a perfected person, i.e., one who has attained nirvāṇa.

awakening
Also called "enlightenment." It is a sudden insight into transcendent, ultimate truth. This is the goal of the Buddha's system of training. After awakening one is free from unnecessary suffering, and after death is free from all suffering. In Buddhist cosmology a fully awakened person, or "arahant," is free from the rounds of rebirth.

Bhante (Pāli)
Literally "Venerable Sir." Although it is a masculine term, it is gender neutral and is used for both monks and nuns.

bhikkhu (Pāli, Sanskrit: bhikṣu)
Literally "beggar." An ordained Buddhist monk. However the term can also refer to anyone following the Buddhist path. When the Buddha gave a talk he would address it to the highest ranking persons there. The rank order was 1) monks, 2) nuns, 3) lay men, and 4) lay women. Thus if even one monk were present, he would address the talk to "bhikkhus."

Bodhisatta (Pāli, Sanskrit: Bodhisattva)
The term used by the Buddha to refer to himself both in his previous lives and as a young man in his current life, prior to his enlightenment, in the period during which he was working towards his own liberation.

deva
In the Buddhist cosmology, devas are gods or heavenly beings that live in the realm just above humans.

Dharma (Sanskrit, Pāli: dhamma)
In Buddhism, the word "dharma" has three different meanings. The first meaning is the universal nature of how things are. At the time of the Buddha, each religious school had its own Dharma, or understanding of how things are. The second meaning of Dharma is the teachings of the Buddha. The third meaning is phenomena. Buddhism sees everything in terms of causes and effects. Mental activities, for example, are dharmas. When referring to the teachings of the Buddha, the word Dharma is capitalized. When referring to phenomena, it is not capitalized.

Dhammapada-aṭṭhakathā ("aṭṭhakathā" is Pāli for *explanation, commentary*)
Commentary to the Dhammapada.

Digha Nikāya
The Long Discourses of the Buddha (Pāli digha = "long"). It is the first of the five *nikāyas*, or collections, in the Sutta Pitaka of the Pāli Canon. Pāli scholar Joy Manné makes the argument that the Digha Nikāya was particularly intended to make converts (Bhikkhu Bodhi pointedly refers to this as "for the purpose of propaganda"!), with its high proportion of debates and devotional material.

Eight Precepts
These are lay precepts for people who want to practice more intensively. They are often observed on Uposatha Days. The additional precepts (to the Five Precepts) are: 1) refrain from eating after noon, 2) refraining from entertainment, wearing jewelry or using perfumes, and 3) sleeping on luxurious beds or over-sleeping.

fetters
Literally a "chain" that shackles one to the rounds of rebirth. The fetters are 1) self-identity view, 2) attachment to rites and rituals, 3) doubt, 4) sense desire, 5) ill will 6) desire for material existence, 7) desire for immaterial existence 8) conceit, 9) restlessness, and 10) ignorance.

Five Faculties
Also called the "Five Strengths" or the "Five Spiritual Faculties." They are 1) faith, 2) energy (vigor/diligence), 3) mindfulness, 4) concentration, and 5) wisdom.

Four Foundations of Mindfulness
Also called the Four Establishings of Mindfulness, and the Four Frames of Reference. The Four Foundations of Mindfulness are 1) the body, 2) feelings, or "feeling tones," 3) mental formations, and 4) mental phenomena.

jhāna (Pāli, Sanskrit: dhyāna)
"meditative absorption." The jhānas are states of high concentration. In the final formulation there are four "material" jhānas and four "immaterial" jhānas.

kōan (Japanese, also *kung-an*)
A kōan is a riddle or puzzle that Zen Buddhists use during meditation to help them unravel a greater truth and break through conceptual thinking.

Majjhima Nikāya
The Middle Length Discourses of the Buddha. It is the second of the five *nikāyas*, or collections, in the Sutta Pitaka of the Pāli Canon. It is generally believed to be the most important collection of discourses in the Canon. The *Majjhima Nikāya* corresponds to the *Madhyama Āgama* which survives in two Chinese translations. Fragments also exist in Sanskrit and Tibetan.

Māra (Pāli, Sanskrit)
Literally "bringer of death." Māra is a deity who embodies the ability of experience, especially sensory experience, to seduce and trap the mind, particularly to prevent the cessation of suffering.

nibbāna (Pāli, Sanskrit: nirvāṇa)
Nibbāna is one of the terms that is used to define the goal of the Buddhist path. It literally means "to extinguish," and means to extinguish the three flames of greed, hatred, and delusion.

non-returner (Pāli, Sanskrit: anāgāmi)
The third of four stages of awakening. A non-returner eliminates the fourth and fifth "fetters" – sense craving and ill-will – and will become an arahant with no more rebirths in the material realm.

once-returner (Pāli: sakadāgāmin, Sanskrit: sakṛdāmin)
The second of four stages of awakening. A once-returner has weakened the fourth and fifth "fetters" – sense craving and ill-will – and will become an arahant with no more than one more rebirth in the material realm.

Pāli Canon

The Pāli Canon is the collection of Buddhist texts preserved in the Pāli language. It consists of three *Pitakas*, or "baskets." These are the *Vinaya Pitaka* (the monastic code), the *Sutta Pitaka* (the discourses of the Buddha and his senior disciples), and the *Abhidhamma Pitaka*, a later work that is variously described as Buddhist philosophy, psychology and metaphysics. The *Abhidhamma Pitaka* is unique to Theravada, or southern, Buddhism; the other collections have versions in the Chinese and Tibetan Canons.

parinibbāna (Pāli, Sanskrit: parinirvāṇa)

Literally "nibbāna after death." When the body of an arahant dies, this frees the being from saṃsara, the rounds of rebirth.

Pātimokkha (Pāli, Sanskrit: Prātimokṣa)

Literally "towards liberation." It is the list of monastic rules in the Vinaya.

Saṇgha (Pāli, Sanskrit: saṃgha)

Literally "community." At the time of the Buddha the term Saṇgha referred either to the community of monastics (monks and nuns) or the noble Saṇgha, which is the community of people who are stream-enterers, once-returners, non-returners, and arahants.

Satipaṭṭhāna (Pāli)

The "Four Foundations of Mindfulness": (1) the body, (2), feelings/sensations, (3) mental formations (thoughts and emotions), and (4) *dharmas*, or phenomena.

Samaṇa (Pāli, Sanskrit: Śramaṇa)

A wandering ascetic.

Saṃyutta Nikāya

The Connected Discourses. It is the third of the five *nikāyas*, or collections, in the Sutta Pitaka of the Pāli Canon. The *Saṃyutta Nikāya* consists of fifty-six chapters, each governed by a unifying theme that binds together the Buddha's suttas or discourses.

Seven Factors of Awakening (enlightenment)

(1) Mindfulness, (2) investigation, (3) energy, (4) joy/rapture, (5) tranquility, (6) concentration, and (7) equanimity.

stream-entry (Pāli: sotāpanna, Sanskrit: srotāpanna)

The first of four stages of awakening. A stream-enterer overcomes the first three "fetters" – self view, attachment to rites and rituals, and skeptical doubt – and will become an arahant in no more than seven lifetimes with no rebirths in the lower realms.

sutta (Pāli, Sanskrit: sutra)
A discourse of the Buddha or one of his disciples. The Pāli word "sutta" refers specifically to the Pāli Canon. The words "sutta" and the Sanskrit form "sutra" literally mean "thread," and are related to the English word "suture."

Tathāgata (Pāli, Sanskrit)
A word the Buddha used when referring to himself. It's literal meaning is ambiguous. It can mean either "thus gone" (tathā-gata) or "thus come" (tathā-āgata). It is probably intentionally ambiguous, meaning that the Buddha, having attained a final awakening, was beyond all comings and goings.

Upāsaka (masculine), **Upāsikā** (feminine) (Pāli, Sanskrit)
Literally "attendant." A lay follower of the Buddha, one who has taken and keeps the Five Precepts.

Uposatha (Pāli, Sanskrit: Upavasatha)
Traditionally held on the new moon and full moon days of the lunar month. This is the day when monastics gather to recite the Pātimokkha (monastic rules) and confess any transgressions. Lay people observe either the Five Precepts or, if they spend the day at a temple or monastery, the Eight Precepts.

Visuddhimagga (Pāli)
Literally, *The Path of Purification*. The *Visuddhimagga* is a Theravada commentarial work attributed to the monk Buddhaghosa, who formulated it in Sri Lanka in the fifth century CE.

Appendix B - Bibliography

Ajahn Lee Dhammadharo (author), Ṭhānissaro Bhikkhu (translator), *Keeping the Breath in Mind & Lessons in Samadhi,* Valley Center: Metta Forest Monastery, 2010.

Ajahn Lee Dhammadharo (author), Ṭhānissaro Bhikkhu (translator), *The Skill of Release, Valley Center: Metta Forest Monastery,* 1995.

Anderson, Bob (author), Anderson, Jean (Illustrator), *Stretching,* Bolinas: Shelter Publications, 2010.

Bhadantacariya Buddhaghosa (Author), Bhikkhu Ñāṇamoli (Translator), *The Path of Purification: Visuddhimagga,* Onalaska: Pariyatti Publishing, 2003.

Bhikkhu Bodhi (Translator), *The Connected Discourses of the Buddha: A Translation of the Saṃyutta Nikāya,* Somerville: Wisdom Publications, 2003.

Bhikkhu Bodhi (Translator), *The Numerical Discourses of the Buddha: A Translation of the Aṇguttara Nikāya,* Somerville: Wisdom Publications, 2012.

Bhikkhu Bodhi, Bhikkhu Khantipalo, Hecker, Hellmuth, Ireland, John D., Norman, K.R., Olendzki, Andrew, Rhys Davids, C.A.F., Sister Khema, *Thera-Therīgāthā: Verses of Arahant Bhikkhus and Bhikkhunīs,* Kandy: Buddhist Publication Society, 2012.

Bhikkhu Ñāṇamoli (Translator), Bhikkhu Bodhi (Translator), *The Middle Length Discourses of the Buddha: A Translation of the Majjhima Nikāya (Teachings of the Buddha),* Somerville: Wisdom Publications, 1995.

Fronsdal, Gil, *The Dhammapada: A New Translation of the Buddhist Classic with Annotations,* Boston & London: Shambhala, 2011.

Rosenberg, Larry, *Breath by Breath: The Liberating Practice of Insight Meditation,* Boston: Shambhala, 2004.

Salzberg, Sharon, *Lovingkindness: The Revolutionary Art of Happiness,* Boston: Shambhala, 2002.

Ṭhānissaro Bhikkhu, *Itivuttaka: This Was Said by the Buddha,* Valley Center: Metta Forest Monastery, 2014.

Ṭhānissaro Bhikkhu, *The Wings to Awakening,* Valley Center: Metta Forest Monastery, 2010.

Ṭhānissaro Bhikkhu, *Udana: Exclamations,* Valley Center: Metta Forest Monastery, 2014.

Ṭhānissaro Bhikkhu, *With Each and Every Breath,* Valley Center: Metta Forest Monastery, 2013.

Thoreau, Henry David, Sanborn, Franklin Benjamin, *Familiar Letters of Henry David Thoreau, Charleston: BiblioLife, 2008.*

Walsh, Maurice (Translator), *The Long Discourses of the Buddha: A Translation of the Digha Nikāya (Teachings of the Buddha),* Somerville: Wisdom Publications, 1995.

32169493R00057

Printed in Great Britain
by Amazon